D0568246

SIMON HOPKINSON

The vegetarian option

Pictures by
JASON LOWE

For Katie, Polly, and George B, and Betsey A,
with love.

◈ Guidelines on using the recipes are given at the end of the introduction, on page 9.

Introduction

One evening in the late summer of 2007 and probably a Sunday, I found myself rummaging around in the salad drawer at the bottom of the refrigerator. Unusually for me, the interior was relatively bare, but all I wanted to eat, anyway, was a bowl of something quick to cook; not really substantial, though nourishing. Two items, slightly the worse for wear, caught my eye: a lone zucchini not yet limp and a package of ready-sliced scarlet runner beans, past their sell-by date by 3 days. There was also the remains of a bunch of parsley. So, I set to work.

I cut the zucchini in half and then into long, thin strips (the most taxing chore of the entire assembly) to mimic the traditional cut of the beans. I briefly boiled both vegetables in salted water until tender, then drained and tossed them into a pan containing a little warming olive oil and sliced garlic. I added a healthy grinding of pepper, stirred everything about a bit, and, finally, sprinkled over it some of the parsley, finely chopped, and turned that through as well. Into a hot bowl it went, and then out with a pair of chopsticks. I ate the dish in about 7 minutes flat,

standing in the kitchen listening to the radio. I cannot begin to tell you how delicious this simple and thrifty affair was, although, I guess, it will not surprise you, as there would have been little point in relating it. As I slipped the empty bowl—licked clean actually, it *was* just me—into a soapy sink, it occurred to me how the dish was complete in itself. It did not need any accompaniment whatsoever, although I suppose a piece of good bread might have been better employed than my tongue in wiping the bowl, but, as I was attempting to not eat bread at the time, the bin was bare.

More important, however, was that I don't think I would have enjoyed it as much if there had been an accompaniment of a cut of meat, a slice of roast chicken, say, or even some lightly steamed fillets of sole. The dish was unique and perfect to that moment. Critically, it also allowed my thoughts to consider quite how easy and adaptable had been my little creation—if you can call it that—without the usual inclusion of my more usual, carnivorous desires.

I shall never be vegetarian. I will reach the age of 55 this year and cannot really see my culinary lifestyle drastically altering any time soon. I am absolutely not going to enter into the world of moral judgment here; I just love all foods. And together with the joy I am given by cooking them, the very idea of restriction of any kind would result in a life not worth living. Incidentally, my reference to "loving all foods" isn't quite true. I do, I'm afraid, deeply loathe the Japanese fermented soybean, known collectively as *natto*. I am not even sure whether the most staunch vegetarian, virgin to such stinking

slime, would countenance these either. But that is about the only comestible I would refuse to put in my mouth. Ironically, it is vegetarian food possibly at its most pure and healthful. Just filthy to eat, that's all. And it is handy to have a dish so readily available when asked of one: "Is there anything you cannot eat?"

As with the delectable dish of zucchini and beans described above, my reasoning for this book is thus: dishes cooked without carnivorous and piscatorial leanings can be every bit as exciting as those with. This has nothing to do with a particular "choice," which is why the title is qualified by one very important word: "option." In the restaurant business, this is the description applied to a dish that will be suitable for vegetarian clients. In my experience, this can be a last-minute request from the head chef to one of his team to "come up with something . . ." And, more often than not, that is exactly how the dish can read on the menu: stir-fried broccoli, tofu, and oyster mushrooms with hazelnut oil might be one example. It may be nice for some, but it isn't for me.

At our London restaurant Bibendum this has never been the case. That which is offered, however, is a thought-out selection of varying, regularly updated, seasonal dishes available from a completely separate, unadvertised menu. For example, when English asparagus comes into season, it will always be there. A salad of green beans might be another. In high summer there will be baked bell peppers with tomatoes and olive oil: "Piedmontese peppers"—a dish with which Bibendum has always been associated —with the usual anchovy fillets omitted for vegetarian guests. And there is a charming story to tell with reference to this.

There was once an American woman dining at the restaurant alone, a vegetarian, who demanded that all the dishes be explained to her in great detail (the à la carte menu is large, to say the least). Finally, she decided upon the Piedmontese peppers, but "without the anchovies, please." Graham Williams, then restaurant manager, complied with this easy request and dispatched the order to the chef in charge of first courses.

On this occasion, the kitchen failed to adhere to Graham's demands and sent out the dish complete with anchovy. The American woman, quite rightly, sent it back. We removed the anchovy and returned the peppers.

The lady tentatively asked "And did you simply remove the anchovies?" Graham's reply was truthful to a tee. "Well, I don't think I can eat this, as it is now tainted. I think I will have the risotto with white truffles instead." "Oh no," Graham expostulated, "you can't possibly eat that. The truffles, at some point, would have been on the end of a pig's nose!" Quite possibly one of the best restaurant tales I know.

÷

Now is the moment to discuss a few guidelines that are useful to know while using this book.

There are several preparations that appear in certain recipes which are used within other dishes, too. For instance: spiced green paste (see page 157); sesame paste (see page 173); ginger syrup (see page 94); Indian masala paste (see page 55); almond & jalapeño relish (see page 99).

As a general rule, use butter that is unsalted or, at least, only slightly salted.

Salt is specified as either "salt" (table salt) or "Maldon sea salt."

Herbs are fresh unless otherwise stated.

Oven timings are for conventional ovens. If you are using a fan-assisted oven, reduce the temperature by 25°F. Use an oven thermometer to check the temperature.

As you will discover, generally I prefer white peppercorns to black. This, however, is entirely a matter for you—and they are not always readily available, either. Sometimes, there is also a sound reasoning as to using white: black specks in mayonnaise, however aromatic their flavor, will always look a bit grubby.

I have also used "agar flakes" in place of the nonvegetarian leaf (or powdered) gelatin, and to great effect, I am pleased to say. Agar flakes are available from some supermarkets and online.

Most of the cheeses used in the book contain the nonvegetarian rennet. I am led to believe that in West Sussex a company called Twineham Grange produces a vegetarian hard cheese allegedly similar to Parmesan, although the powers that be in Parma, Italy, would no doubt furiously (and probably rightly) contest such a comparison. You may be able to find other vegetarian cheeses in supermarkets or online— I leave it to you to search them out.

Finally, I have given two recipes for stock: one a delicious vegetable bouillon, the other a simple chicken broth. In all recipes I simply refer to "stock," rather than specify as to which one.

The option, as ever, is yours.

SIMON HOPKINSON, APRIL 2009

Bouillon

It was at Marc Meneau's L'Espérance, in Saint-Père-sous-Vézelay, northern Burgundy, that I first tasted a fine vegetable "bouillon." It was high summer, around the end of July, 1985. The bouillon was poured at table, chilled—nay, ice cold—into a glass soup plate ready garnished with a dice of jewellike vegetables. It was exactly what was needed after the journey from Paris in a rented car without air-conditioning.

Well, I had never eaten anything like it! As Michelin had bestowed their coveted three stars upon the restaurant, I suppose one would have expected something startling. But quite how Chef Meneau had managed to infuse such intensive flavor into that which resembled nothing more than a clear, pale yellow, watery liquid was difficult to understand. I almost wanted to drink this elixir without interruption from the floating pieces of vegetable, it was so good.

The secret, I discovered, was to cook the bouillon in a preserving jar such as those made by Le Parfait or Ball; and I do honestly believe that this method gives the best results. However, I have also experimented with a pressure cooker,

for about 30 minutes, with good results, but the intensity of flavor here versus the original method is slightly less full and less clean tasting. I would suggest that if you are using the bouillon as the star of a dish, it is worth using the preserving jar method. Otherwise, just simmer everything in a covered stainless steel pan on very low heat, for about 1½ hours.

You may want a stronger flavored bouillon for soups, sauces, a risotto, say, where clarity and finesse are less important. If so, I suggest that as you strain the stock through a fine strainer, you press as much juice from the vegetable debris with the back of a ladle as you can.

Conversely, for the finest clear vegetable bouillon, strain through a cheesecloth-lined sieve and leave to drain without pressure. Even then, you may perceive the merest collection of base deposit. If so, simply allow the bouillon to settle and then carefully decant into another container, leaving the sediment behind.

The recipe provided (overleaf) uses the Meneau preserving jar method, but the choice of flavoring ingredients is mine.

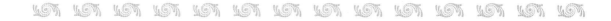

My vegetable bouillon (stock)

makes about 1½ quarts

◈ Please note that these instructions are for the Le Parfait jars; if you are using a different kind of preserving jar, please use the method recommended by the manufacturer. Throughout the book, this bouillon will simply be referred to as "stock."

¾ cup peeled and chopped carrots

1 cup chopped and well washed leeks, both green and white parts

¾ cup chopped celery

1 cup thinly sliced white button mushrooms

2 cups peeled and chopped white onion

1 cup chopped ripe tomato

3 garlic cloves, halved

3 bay leaves

handful of parsley sprigs, roughly chopped

21 black peppercorns

3 teaspoons Maldon sea salt

about 6 cups water

You will need three scrupulously washed 3-cup (750ml)-capacity Le Parfait or other preserving jars (see above). You will also need to use a pan that is deep enough to take the jars and almost immerse them in water. It is worth placing a thickly folded sheet of newspaper in the bottom, or a small piece of cardboard underneath each jar, to prevent an, albeit rare, cracking of the glass. (I use a cooktop metal heat-diffuser as a trivet.)

Thoroughly mix the vegetables and tomato together in a roomy bowl. Now, half-fill the preserving jars with the vegetables and then equally distribute the garlic, herbs, and peppercorns among them. Add the remaining vegetables and then add 1 teaspoon salt to each jar. Add the water, stopping about ¾ inch from the top. Seal the jars.

Place the jars in the pan and add cold water until it almost reaches the lids. Slowly bring up to a very gentle simmer, then cover and cook for 2 hours, topping off with boiling water from a kettle whenever the volume has visibly dropped. Once the 2 hours is up, allow the bouillon to cool completely in the water.

Either store until needed (keep in the refrigerator for safety, even though sterilized) or break the seal and strain the bouillon there and then. Discard the vegetables; they have done their work. Of course, once strained, the bouillon may successfully be frozen in small, plastic pots.

Chicken broth (stock)

makes about 2 quarts

❖ As far as I know, I will remain a carnivore for the foreseeable future. So, for those of similar inclination who wish to continue using a poultry-based stock for soups and risottos, for instance, this chicken broth is here for you. Use it, if you like, instead of the vegetable bouillon (opposite), wherever "stock" is listed in a recipe.

2 pounds chicken wings or drumsticks, roughly chopped

3 quarts water

3 celery stalks, chopped

3 leeks, trimmed, chopped, and well washed

1 medium carrot, peeled and chopped

2 small onions, peeled and chopped

3 garlic cloves, bashed

4 ripe tomatoes, peeled and chopped

1 chicken stock cube

3 thyme sprigs

2 bay leaves

8 black peppercorns

6 parsley sprigs

2 teaspoons Maldon sea salt

Put the wings or drumsticks into a large pan, add the water, and bring up to a simmer. Skim off any resultant gray scum, then add all the other ingredients and stir. Bring up to a simmer once more, remove any further scum (from the vegetables), and then cook slowly, just with the merest "blips" bubbling on the surface, for about 2 hours.

Pour the stock through a colander into a clean pan and let drain and drip for 15 minutes. Remove any fat from the surface with several paper towels, then pour through a fine strainer into a bowl. Cool and then ladle into jars. Put lids on and keep in the refrigerator, where they will keep for 4 to 5 days, or freeze in plastic containers.

Tomatoes & Olive Oil

The finest tomatoes I have ever had the pleasure of both using and eating are those locally grown in the Mani region, on the Peloponnese peninsula in southern Greece. So heavy are these with sweet, fragrant flesh and juice, occasional fruits have weighed more than 1½ pounds each! Of course, simply sliced and dressed with olive oil (again local, naturally) they are at their most superb and beautiful to behold, with their sparkling seeds pocketed within thick, meaty partitions. I particularly enjoy eating them with some thinly sliced onions, which, in Greece, are a lovely pale pink, mild, and sweet; plus the olive oil, of course. And, finally, my perfect breakfast is a thick slice of tomato, slowly fried in olive oil, with a fried egg (from the butcher's wife) popped on top. I call it "my small Greek breakfast."

Cooked, these gorgeous toms behave quite magnificently. The English friends who have invited me into their Greek holiday home enjoy a Bloody Mary as much as I do, so we make our own fresh tomato juice. The tomatoes, however, need to be slightly cooked, as simply making a purée of raw tomatoes will give you only a sort of pink pap. Given time, this would separate out into an unattractive suspension of pulp and pale, thin juice. So, core the tomatoes, blanch in boiling water for a few seconds, and then peel (although this step is not essential, I sometimes wonder if the skins contribute bitterness, once cooked). Cut them up into rough chunks and put into a large, stainless steel pan with a little salt and a pinch of sugar; if the tomatoes are naturally sweet then this will probably be unnecessary. Add a little water to start the cooking process and put on low heat.

The trick here is to take the process only until the tomatoes have given off most of their juice, but still remain a touch undercooked. If heated too much, the juice tastes of cooked tomatoes, and again, once cooled and allowed to settle, it is likely to separate. Now, force the mixture through a coarse strainer using the back of a ladle, or, better still, through a food mill, then pass this through a finer sieve to remove the seeds. Job done. Keep in a screw-top bottle in the refrigerator, where it will stay fresh for 4 to 5 days. Shake well before use.

I buy my everyday olive oil from Andrew Carmichael, an esteemed veterinary surgeon in Holland Park, West London, who also happens to be the proprietor of an olive grove estate on the island of Crete. It is very good extra-virgin oil indeed and excellent value.

However, two very particular olive oils—one from Tuscany, the other from Provence—need special mention. The Italian one is Cappezana, from a medieval estate that has been producing olive oil since A.D. 804. This I only ever use for fine dressings or spooning over thick slices of fresh mozzarella, or its creamy cousin burrata. I would also use it to dress the choicest sliced tomatoes, on the rare occasion that I may find them in West London, on a warm summer's day.

The French oil is from Le Moulin de Jean-Marie Cornille, in the village of Maussane-les-Alpilles, near St. Rèmy de Provence, but is generally known simply as *Huile de Maussane*. I know of no other oil as fragrantly pungent as this one, although it has a refinement and individuality that, for me, are unique. When used to make golden aïoli, it is peerless.

Tomato jelly with basil & goat cheese

serves 4

❖ Before writing this book, I had never needed to use a vegetarian gelling agent, namely agar-agar, although I knew vaguely of its seaweed origins, so highly prized in Japan. In Ireland, carragheen moss, a different variety of seaweed, is used for the purpose, notably in the pudding known, not surprisingly, as Carragheen moss pudding. I had no idea of the setting properties of agar-agar or, clearly, how much to use. On using it, I discovered that the instructions on the package gave a set that was very much too firm; well, for me, it was. I spent a great deal of time experimenting with the set, and the resultant delicate texture achieved in the following recipe is one of enormous finesse, melting in the mouth in the nicest possible way. Agar flakes, however, will not produce a crystal-clear jelly in the way conventional gelatin leaves do. Or, at least, they didn't for me. However, an agar jelly has the advantage that it does not form a skin. Note that it will eventually set at room temperature, too.

¾ cup stock

2 heaping teaspoons agar flakes

1 pound ripest tomatoes (cherry, small plum, or very ripe summer tomatoes), minced or processed to a mush

1 scant teaspoon Maldon sea salt

1 scant teaspoon sugar

pinch of dried chili flakes

¼ pound soft goat cheese

1 heaped tablespoon sour cream

1 small clove garlic, crushed to a paste with a little Maldon sea salt

small handful of basil leaves, minced

freshly ground white pepper

Put the stock into a stainless steel pan, sprinkle the agar flakes over, but do not stir in. Allow to come up to a gentle simmer and then swirl the pan around over the heat, until the flakes begin to melt. Simmer for 3 to 4 minutes and then add the tomatoes, salt, sugar, and chili. Bring up to just under simmering point and then pass through a fine strainer suspended over a bowl. Initially, simply allow the juice to drip through, then carefully move the tomato pulp around with a spoon to coax more juice out, but do not force or press it.

Meanwhile, thoroughly mix the goat cheese, sour cream, garlic, basil, and pepper together in a bowl. Spoon into the base of four small glass tumblers (or similar), dividing it equally.

Now take the bowl of tomato liquid and place it over a larger bowl filled with ice cubes and water. Taking a metal spoon, gently stir the liquid around until it just begins to gel; this will take about 10 minutes, but note that when it starts to gel, it will happen quite swiftly.

Spoon the jelly over the cheese mixture and refrigerate for about 1 hour. The jellies are best eaten there and then. Serve with teaspoons and eat with thin, hot, buttered toast. An elegant summer first course, best eaten out of doors.

Tomato salad with basil cream dressing *&* olive oil

serves 2

I first recall eating tomato salad with a cream dressing at the Italian restaurant Montpeliano, in London's Knightsbridge. It must have been in the late 1970s, soon after I had first arrived in London. When the salad arrived, we were somewhat surprised to receive two large white plates covered with ripest red, sliced tomatoes, anointed with a generous dressing of what looked like heavy cream. That was until we tasted it. Ice cold and almost sweet and sour, this cream dressing was just fabulous. Freshly torn basil leaves, a grinding of pepper from the handsome waiter (giant mills all the rage then), and a trickle of good olive oil shining in rivulets upon its creamy surface . . . Just perfect.

1 ½ tablespoons white wine vinegar

2 tablespoons warm water

Maldon sea salt and freshly ground pepper

⅓ cup whipping cream

¼ cup (scant) extra-virgin olive oil, plus a little extra

pinch of sugar

7 or 8 basil leaves, torn or chopped

4 ripe, medium-small tomatoes, cored and sliced

In a mixing bowl, whisk together the wine vinegar, water, and seasoning until combined. Now whisk in the cream, olive oil, and sugar until well amalgamated, then stir in the basil.

Lay the tomatoes onto a large plate (preferably white), very lightly season, and spoon the dressing over. Trickle a little extra olive oil over and serve directly.

Homemade tomato sauce

makes about 1 quart

◈ This sauce is always good to have on hand . . . and it freezes well, too.

4½ pounds ripe tomatoes, peeled

1 head of garlic, each clove peeled and then bruised

2 bay leaves

leaves from 1 head of green celery, or 2 celery stalks, chopped

thinly pared rind of 1 small lemon

2 teaspoons sugar

a little salt

Roughly chop the tomatoes and put them into a heavy-bottomed pan. Add all the other ingredients and bring to a simmer. Allow to cook very, very gently for 1½ to 2 hours, stirring from time to time. As the final sauce consistency should be a bit sloppy and still just pourable, take the pan from the heat before the sauce looks too thick.

Personally, I like to first use a food mill, using the finest disk, and then further force the resultant sauce through a fine strainer, pressing down well with the back of a small ladle.

Baked stuffed tomatoes "paella style"

serves 4

❖ Although the flavors in this dish are those of Spanish paella, the rice I have chosen is Italian carnaroli; other risotto rice may be employed (a simple arborio or vialone nano), but I find carnaroli swells more evenly and tenderly for the stuffing.

These tomatoes may also be served alongside other small dishes as part of a buffet lunch (in which case, one each is sufficient). For a first course, as here, you will need two.

8 firm, ripe medium–small tomatoes

½ small green bell pepper, seeded, pith removed, and coarsely chopped

4 garlic cloves, peeled and crushed

large pinch of dried chili flakes

handful of Italian parsley leaves

1 teaspoon Spanish paprika

1 teaspoon saffron threads, steeped in 1 tablespoon boiling water

½ cup olive oil, plus a little more, if liked

⅓ cup carnaroli rice

Maldon sea salt

Remove the stalks from the tomatoes and then turn them over. Using a small, sharp knife, slice through about a fifth of the way down the tomato, to give little caps. Reserve these for later. Now, using a teaspoon, carefully scoop out all of the tomato innards into a bowl. Place the hollowed-out shells in a roasting dish that will accommodate them snugly.

Put the green bell pepper, garlic, chili, parsley, paprika, and infused saffron (with its water) into a food processor and pulse until the ingredients are evenly but coarsely chopped. Now tip in the tomato pulp with a generous ⅓ cup of the olive oil and process further until the entire mixture is a sloppy, seedy, and oily tomato pap, with the other solids now more finely processed and in suspension.

Put the rice into the bowl that previously held the tomato pulp. Pour the tomato pap from the food processor over it, mix well, and season with salt to taste. Leave to soak for 30 minutes, stirring occasionally. Preheat the oven to 400°F.

Fill the tomatoes with the rice mixture. Don't be tempted to overfill—there may be a little left over—but do make sure that as much liquid as possible is included, even if it overflows into the dish. Replace the little caps onto the tomatoes and trickle the remaining oil over (plus a little more, if you like).

Bake in the oven for about 45 minutes, turning the heat down a touch if the tomatoes are browning too much—but browned and blistered they certainly must be! Taste a little of the rice to make sure it is fully cooked, although it will also continue to swell and tenderize as it cools. Serve at room temperature, for preference, basting well with the juices and oil just before serving.

Asparagus & Artichokes

When they overlap, this pair is one of the great green treats of early summer. At Secretts Farm, near Godalming, Surrey, on a sunny Saturday morning, you can often find me striding between the well-kept rows of asparagus spears, with trusty sharp knife and basket. I am like a child indulging in a brand-new craze over and over again, and love this excellent place for allowing me this simple pleasure. And there is a further bonus on the way back from the asparagus beds—a whole field given over to globe artichokes. Joy of joys!

A few years back, and for a couple of years, or so, Secretts had to call a halt to pick-your-own asparagus because a significant number of pickers had, how shall we say, been unscrupulous with their cutting skills—or lack of, I guess. This ignorant behavior involved simply cutting off the asparagus tips, rather than removing entire spears, as more thoughtful and respectful pickers are moved to do. Mind you, it is how most asparagus—especially that out of season—is sold in supermarkets. Perhaps that is all these bewildered folk know.

I see choosing and picking my own asparagus as not just a joy but the choicest luxury, and like to pick the biggest, fattest spears. To be deprived of such a brief, seasonal pleasure is saddening. So, please be kind and respectful of this excellent enterprise—and of the asparagus, too—so it may continue year in, year out.

Traditionally cut asparagus should include the white base beneath the soil. Once well washed, these may be used along with the peel from the stalks to make wonderful asparagus soups—to be enjoyed either hot or chilled. Rice is the most successful thickener here, as potatoes can sometimes produce a gluey texture. A good asparagus soup should be limpidly smooth, a lovely pale green (from the skins added late in the cooking process), and with just a touch of cream added as a final enrichment. Tarragon or chervil is a good herb to employ as a secondary flavor.

A final thought concerning asparagus. There are those who insist that English asparagus is the finest in the world. I think it is wonderful too, but I would argue that all asparagus, absolutely freshly picked anywhere in the world and plunged promptly into a pan of fast-boiling salted water to cook for several minutes, will taste just as fine. Freshness, with asparagus, is all.

The artichokes grown at Secretts are the large, Breton variety, rather than the smaller, softer, and purple-leafed variety most synonymous with Italy—and the Veneto, in particular. Here, in March and April, there are tiny artichokes in the Rialto market harvested from the islands of the lagoon. These are known as *castraure*, which literally translates as "taken out from" (with connotations of castration).

The first tiny bud is cut out from the very center of the plant, allowing future, larger artichokes to flourish through the summer—as many as twenty per plant. They are not cheap, but such a short season never is. At Harry's Bar, six are trimmed to the size of small corks, baked with olive oil, and simply served warm on a small plate. So delicious are they, I eat them very slowly using my fingers, while momentarily forgetting that they might possibly cost the price of ten pizzas, the other side of San Marco. Then again, what would I want with ten pizzas?

Warm asparagus custards with tarragon vinaigrette

serves 4

✽ The texture of these little darlings is wonderfully wobbly and delicate, so do take the greatest care when the moment of optimum set is reached. Practice makes perfect, as with all crucial cookery skills.

for the custards

½ pound asparagus

salt

a little softened butter for greasing the ramekins

2 large eggs

2 large egg yolks

½ cup whipping cream

Maldon sea salt and freshly ground white pepper

for the vinaigrette

1 tablespoon tarragon vinegar

1 teaspoon Dijon mustard

salt and freshly ground pepper

2 tablespoons sunflower oil

3 tablespoons extra–virgin olive oil

2 teaspoons minced tarragon leaves

Trim the stalk ends of the asparagus and peel the lower part of the stems, then cut the spears into short lengths. Cook them in boiling, well-salted water until a touch more than just tender, drain, and immediately plunge into a bowl of water chilled with plenty of ice cubes. Leave until quite cold, then lift out and carefully, but thoroughly, dry in a dish towel. The asparagus will then be ready to use.

Preheat the oven to 300°F. Butter four ramekins and line the base of each with a tiny disk of waxed paper.

Put the cooked asparagus into a blender with the eggs and egg yolks and purée until really smooth. Pour into a fine strainer suspended over a bowl and, with aid of a small ladle, force through as much mixture as possible. Stir the cream into the purée until well mixed and season with a little salt and pepper to taste. Pour the mixture into the prepared ramekins, filling them to just below the brim.

Cover each with a circle of foil and place in a deep baking dish. Pour tap-hot water into the dish until it comes at least three-quarters of the way up the sides of the molds. Bake in the oven for 25 to 30 minutes, or until just firm to the touch. Leave to cool until warm, but no cooler.

Meanwhile, make the vinaigrette. Simply mix together the vinegar, mustard, and seasoning in a small bowl, then whisk in the oils until emulsified (add a tiny splash of hot water to aid this, if you like). Stir in the tarragon.

To serve, spoon a little of the vinaigrette onto the surface of each custard. Eat with strips of hot buttered toast.

Asparagus with olive oil & blood orange butter sauce

serves 2

❖ The dressing employed in this dish is an oily version of the butter-rich sauce known as "Maltaise." It is unusually diverting.

1 large bunch of asparagus (about 14 to 16 spears)

salt

for the sauce

2 large egg yolks

grated zest and juice of 2 blood oranges

5 tablespoons unsalted butter, melted and kept warm

⅓ cup extra-virgin olive oil

Maldon sea salt and freshly ground white pepper

squeeze of lemon juice, to taste

To make the sauce, place the egg yolks in a glass bowl with the orange juice and zest and suspend the bowl over a pan of barely simmering water, making sure it is not touching the water. Whisk over the heat for several minutes until the mixture is thick and glossy; be careful not to overcook it or the eggs will scramble.

Remove from the heat and slowly whisk in the butter until incorporated, leaving behind the milky residue for the time being; if the finished sauce is too thick, some of this may later be added to thin it slightly. Now whisk in the olive oil, season, and add the lemon juice. The consistency of the sauce should be similar to a loose mayonnaise—pourable, yet wobbly. Strain the sauce through a fine strainer into a warmed bowl (to rid the sauce of the orange zest).

Trim the asparagus bases and peel the lower end of the stalks. Add to a pan of boiling well-salted water and boil for about 5 minutes, or until tender when pierced with a sharp knife. *Please* don't undercook the asparagus, as I think there is nothing worse; the spears should just give to the teeth. Once cooked, lift them out with a slotted spoon and drain on a dish towel. Divide between two warm plates and hand the sauce separately at table.

Warm salad of asparagus & new potatoes

serves 4

◇ A pleasure of both texture and seasonality is the general idea here.

¾ pound new potatoes, scrupulously scraped or peeled

salt

2 large mint sprigs

2 scant tablespoons unsalted butter

½ pound asparagus tips

hearts of 2 Boston lettuces, leaves separated, washed, and carefully dried

Maldon sea salt

2 hard-boiled eggs, shelled

handful of chervil sprigs

for the butter sauce

juice of 1 lemon

pinch of superfine sugar

5 tablespoons cold unsalted butter, cut into small chunks

freshly ground white pepper

1 tablespoon chopped chives

Simmer the potatoes in lightly salted water just to cover, with the mint, until tender. Drain over another pan or bowl, keep the water for now, and return the potatoes to the pan with the butter. Stir together, cover, and keep warm.

For the sauce, take a roomy and shallow, stainless steel or enameled saucepan and squeeze in the lemon juice. Add 6 tablespoons of the potato cooking water and the sugar, then simmer this mixture until reduced by half. Now slowly incorporate the butter, one chunk at a time, whisking over a thread of heat until limpid and homogenous (this is essentially a light butter sauce). Season with pepper. Again, keep warm.

Peel the asparagus tips from just below the bud and slice them in half lengthwise. Add to a pan of boiling well-salted water and boil rapidly for about 1 to 2 minutes (eat one to see if they are cooked; they should be just tender, not almost raw), then drain.

Slice the warm potatoes and add these, together with the asparagus, to the butter sauce. Turn them gently through the sauce with the chives, until all are evenly coated.

Arrange the lettuce leaves on four plates and divide the asparagus and potatoes between them. Sprinkle with a little Maldon sea salt and judiciously grate the egg over. Generously scatter over chervil sprigs, which are not there just to look pretty; their faint anise flavor is very pleasing.

Asparagus frittata with soft cheese & chives

serves 2

◈ This would be a fine opportunity to use asparagus spears known as "sprue," which are much thinner and, consequently, less expensive than more perfect specimens. If so, do not bother to peel them; just remove the tougher base stalks.

½ pound asparagus

1 tablespoon olive oil

salt and cayenne pepper

scant scraping of freshly grated nutmeg

3 large eggs, beaten

½ cup soft cream cheese

¼ cup finely grated Parmesan

2 teaspoons chopped chives

a thin slice of butter

Trim the asparagus bases, peel the lower end of the stalks, and thinly slice the spears on the diagonal. Warm the olive oil in a nonstick skillet, add the asparagus, and season with salt, cayenne pepper, and nutmeg. Cook gently over low heat until the asparagus are tender and very lightly colored; eat a sliver to see if it is cooked through. Tip out onto a plate, set aside, and wipe out the skillet.

In a mixing bowl, beat together the eggs, cream cheese, Parmesan, and chives until smooth. Return the skillet to moderate heat, add the butter, and heat until just beginning to froth. Pour in the egg mixture, turn down the heat to low, and then quietly begin to bring in the frothing edges to the liquid center of the pan using a spatula.

Now tip in the cooked asparagus and carefully disperse evenly. Continue to gently lift the more cooked parts of the frittata, so allowing the liquid egg to slip underneath until a soft and curdlike texture has evolved—this should take no more than 2 minutes, or so.

Slide the frittata onto a plate and eat warm or at room temperature, but certainly not hot from the pan.

Globe artichoke, fava bean & pea stew

serves 4

◈ Do not be concerned as to the dull green look of the finished dish. This is what happens when such vegetables are given a slow-cooked treatment.

4 to 5 tablespoons extra-virgin olive oil

6 to 8 scallions, trimmed and sliced

2 or 3 garlic cloves, peeled and sliced

1 teaspoon fennel seeds, crushed slightly with a pestle and mortar

3 tablespoons dry vermouth

½ pound artichoke hearts (fresh or frozen), cut into small wedges

¾ pound shelled fava beans

¾ pound shelled peas

⅓ cup water

salt and freshly ground pepper

2 tablespoons chopped mint

squeeze of lemon juice (optional)

Warm 2 to 3 tablespoons of the olive oil in a solid, roomy pot. Add the scallions, garlic, and fennel seeds and gently soften until translucent and limp. Pour in the vermouth, allow to bubble for a minute or two, then put in the artichoke hearts. Cover and allow to stew over low heat for about 15 to 20 minutes, stirring occasionally.

Now add the fava beans and peas, with another 1 tablespoon olive oil, and continue to cook, covered, for another 5 minutes. Add the water, seasoning, and another 1 tablespoon of oil and stir all together. Cover with a circle of waxed paper, put on the lid, and continue stewing, very, very gently, until the vegetables are well cooked and no longer bright green. Only now is the dish almost ready. It is important that the vegetables be well cooked; it is a stew, after all. Reckon on about 45 to 50 minutes' gentle cooking time in all.

Now add the mint and, if you like, the lemon juice. Spoon into a handsome serving dish (preferably white), adding just a trickle more oil over the surface. Serve at room temperature to enjoy the dish at its best.

Globe artichoke soup

serves 4

◈ Consider making this soup only if you have access to ready-prepared artichoke hearts, either frozen (available from selected supermarkets), or fresh if you happen to be staying in Italy—almost always there will be a vendor in the local market with trays of prepared artichoke hearts bobbing about in acidulated water, which he will gladly sell you. Choose the cheapest ones available, as they vary in price from perfect to scraps. Clearly, here, the latter will be perfectly acceptable.

The flavor of the soup is impeccable in its delicacy and may, of course, be consumed without the luxury of thin shavings of black truffle over its surface, once decanted into warmed, shallow soup plates. There again, the wider the plate, the greater the area of possible abundance. So, if you are lucky enough to have access to such rare bounty, shave away to your heart's content.

2 tablespoons olive oil

½ pound leeks, trimmed, sliced, and washed

1¼ pounds artichoke hearts (fresh or frozen), chopped

2 garlic cloves, crushed and chopped

salt and freshly ground white pepper

2 cups stock

1½ cups milk

3 tablespoons butter

⅓ cup whipping cream

fresh black truffle (optional)

Heat the olive oil in a roomy pan, add the leeks, and stew until softened. Add the artichokes and garlic, stir around for a few moments, then season and pour in the stock and milk. Bring up to a simmer, cover, and cook gently for about 30 to 40 minutes, or until the artichokes are very tender and almost falling apart. Do not worry about the split appearance of the liquid, it will be resolved at the next stage.

Now process the mixture in a blender until very smooth indeed. Pass through a fine strainer back into the (wiped-clean) pan, and then whisk in the butter and cream, while keeping the soup hot over medium heat. Once all is ready and velvety smooth, pour into heated soup plates and thinly shave over it some black truffle—or not, as the case may be.

Cauliflower & Broccoli

When a freshly harvested cauliflower is in the peak of condition I gain great pleasure in running my hand over its creamy white curds, almost completely enclosed by sturdy, green leafy ribs, still wet with rainwater or morning dew. Granted, it is only at the very best farm shops where this is ever likely to happen, but the experience is a special one—well, it is for me. There is always something wonderful when encountering really fresh produce—be it organic or otherwise—and the cauliflower takes some beating in this respect.

Maybe this is because cauliflower is often seen as something rather mundane in the panoply of "world" vegetables that are now so readily available to most of us. Often, in fact, the more ordinary the produce, the more I become excited when I discover it in excellent condition.

To carefully pry apart crisp florets of the freshest cauliflower and turn them into a deliciously comforting cauliflower and cheese (see page 34), is one of the nicest initial preparations, particularly when one knows that, once boiled until just tender, they are going to be blanketed in the very best cheese sauce one can possibly muster. All such thrills matter to the caring cook who loves to eat good things.

Dear old broccoli is no different in its ubiquity, except that it appears in more varied guises. In Italy and the United States, broccoli rabe, with small florets and jagged leaves, is a favorite. Here in Britain pile upon pile of purple sprouting broccoli is the treat of mid-February into mid-April—the native harvest, that is. Some years ago I was staying on the Suffolk coast and made a slight detour to Alder Carr Farmers' Market, just on the edge of the village of Needham Market, on my route back to London.

My arrival happily coincided with a tractor returning from the land with a truck attached that was, astonishingly, laden with what looked like an entire field of purple sprouting broccoli. Although there was plenty of broccoli in the market, I excitedly insisted that I would like mine fresh from the tractor. Eager to please this grown-up child, they duly allowed me to choose my bounty. Naturally, I purchased much more than I needed. So, both parties satisfied.

To briefly return to those cauliflowers, one of the most delicious, almost-instant soups can be made using small florets of cauliflower. Quickly boil them in a lightly flavored stock until really quite soft, together with several thinly sliced scallions, white part only. Add a knob of butter, then blitz in a blender until super-smooth. Strain through a fine sieve and serve in piping hot soup bowls, with a spoonful or two of cream floated on the surface. The fresh taste of this lily-white soup is especially fine and should not be subjected to reheating. Eat with tiny, buttery croutons.

Cauliflower & cheese

serves 2, generously

◈ Personally, I generally use tasty Lancashire for my cauliflower and cheese, as that is what my mother always bought from the local market. But any good, firm cheese will do fine, such as Cheddar, Parmesan, or Gruyère.

1 cauliflower

salt and freshly ground white pepper

2 cups whole milk

2 cloves

1 small onion, peeled and chopped

1 bay leaf

5 tablespoons butter

⅓ cup (scant) all-purpose flour

1⅔ cups grated firm cheese, plus a little extra for sprinkling on top

a little freshly grated nutmeg

Remove the green leaves from the cauliflower and break the curds into roughly even-size florets. Add the cauliflower florets to a pan of boiling salted water and boil until almost tender (remember, they will continue to cook while in the sauce, in the oven). Drain and carefully lay out on a folded dish towel; their cooking water will continue to exude for quite some minutes after draining.

Preheat the oven to 375°F. Put the milk, cloves, onion, and bay leaf in a small saucepan and bring up to a simmer. Cook for a minute or two, then cover and leave to infuse off the heat for 10 minutes or so.

In another pan, melt the butter and stir in the flour. Cook, stirring, over low heat for a few minutes, then remove from the heat and strain in the hot milk all at once. Whisk together vigorously until well amalgamated. Now, using a wooden spoon, stir continuously until the sauce begins to thicken and become very smooth. Leave to cook for another 10 minutes over the merest heat; one of those heat-diffuser mats employed here would be a good idea. Add the cheese and stir until it has fully melted into the sauce. Season with pepper and nutmeg and taste for salt.

Place the cauliflower in an ovenproof dish that will accommodate it snugly. Carefully pour the sauce over so that it fully coats each floret and sprinkle with the extra cheese. Bake in the oven for a good 25 to 30 minutes, or until the surface is well blistered and the sauce is bubbling nicely around the edges.

Broccoli with courchamps sauce

serves 2

❄ A most delicious sauce, this one, and adapted from a recipe in Elizabeth David's *An Omelette and a Glass of Wine*. Unique and unusual, it really is not the same if you forgo the anisette. Although available only in a large bottle, it keeps for ages. I think I have had mine for at least 10 years.

¾ pound broccoli rabe

salt

for the sauce

2 or 3 bushy tarragon sprigs

3 or 4 parsley sprigs

2 shallots, peeled and coarsely chopped

freshly ground pepper

1 teaspoon Dijon mustard

2 teaspoons anisette (or Pernod or Pastis)

juice of ½ small lemon

2 teaspoons light soy sauce

4 tablespoons extra-virgin olive oil, or more if needed

Trim the broccoli well and cook in boiling salted water until tender.

For the sauce, pick the leaves from the herb sprigs and place them in a small blender with all the other ingredients. Purée until smooth. Taste the sauce and see if you need any more oil, or indeed, a little salt or more soy sauce. Pour into a small serving bowl.

Drain the broccoli as soon as it is cooked and serve at once, using fingers to dip the stalks in the sauce.

Broccoli with chopped egg & sherry bread crumbs

serves 2

❄ Sharp, buttery, and crunchy textures. A surprisingly comforting assembly.

5 tablespoons butter

⅔ cup fresh white bread crumbs

salt and freshly ground pepper

2 tablespoons Amontillado sherry

1 large head of broccoli, broken up into small florets

2 hard-boiled eggs, chopped (or grated, if you like)

1½ tablespoons sherry vinegar

Heat half of the butter in a pan until frothing and add the bread crumbs, salt, and pepper. Fry gently until all the butter has been soaked up and allow to color for a few minutes, then pour in the sherry. Once the frothing has subsided, you will notice that the mixture has become sticky. Don't worry, just turn down the heat and stir fairly constantly with a wooden spoon until lumps begin to collect. In time, about 15 minutes, these will break back down into crumbs, the sherry having been driven off by evaporation—its flavor left behind with the browned butter. The crumbs should be crisp and golden. Keep them warm.

Boil the broccoli in salted water until tender and drain well. Pile neatly into a hot serving dish and strew the crumbs and chopped egg over. Heat the remaining butter in a small pan until it begins to turn golden and smell nutty. Remove from the heat, wait a few seconds, and then spoon in the vinegar, which will froth and splutter. Swirl the fat and liquid together to loosely amalgamate and then spoon over the broccoli. Serve without delay.

Pumpkin & Squash

I would reckon that many pumpkins sold in Britain remain uneaten, as they are only ever really seen in greengrocers—and supermarkets, most definitely—in the weeks leading up to Hallowe'en. Then again, I may be wrong. But at this festive occasion, they are first emptied of their flesh (consumed? . . . I think not), a spooky face cut into the tough skin, and a small candle placed inside. This is certainly not the case in the United States. While sales of pumpkin must also surely rocket during the month of October, with similar faces cut into their tough skin, pumpkins are also hugely popular at the American table, as well as flickering on the windowsill.

However, that which seems to be the most prevalent dish made from pumpkin in the United States has always been a problem with me. That Pie. I just don't understand it. I can only hope that one day some extraordinarily brilliant American cook will present me with a slice of one that I can at least finish. Be that as it may, I love lots of American food. Maryland crab cakes, oysters Rockefeller, shad roe in early spring, fabulous juicy steaks, southern fried chicken,

pastrami on rye, lox and bagels are all wonderful. Then there is the irresistible fudgy-textured New York cheese-cake, the one that is "clarty"—a Lancashire expression to describe food that sticks to the roof of your mouth. And, of course, the truly scrummy pecan pie.

I came to like squash—and butternut in particular—relatively late in my culinary life. To be honest, at first I gave it the same short shrift as pumpkin. I recall the other pumpkin recipe that I was always polite about and consumed dutifully. It was a soup that Mum used to make occasionally toward the end of her life. I never knew quite why she bothered, as it was forever and absolutely bereft of taste. Curious, that, as her other dishes rarely failed to delight.

Anyway, squash is good. Baked butternut doused with olive oil and dressed with lemon juice (see page 42) is simple and delicious. The ravioli derivative that follows (on page 43) takes a little more time and effort, but is well worth the journey. And the pumpkin soup (overleaf) might just convince one that there is more to this vegetable than Hallowe'en lanterns.

Pumpkin soup "Paul Bocuse"

serves about 4

◇ I first encountered this curious, slightly hit-and-miss recipe in the back pages of the seminal book *Great Chefs of France*, by Quentin Crewe and Anthony Blake (tragically now out of print). It is the only book I have ever read cover to cover in one sitting—or one lying, in fact, as I devoured it through the night. Here is the original, word for word, as part of Bocuse's annual New Year greeting cards sent to friends:

SOUPE DE COURGE À LA CRÈME

"The pumpkin is a vegetable which it is wrong to neglect. One can make gratins and soup with it. Here is a delicious recipe. Cut the top off a 4 to 5 kilo pumpkin so that it looks like a soup bowl. Scoop out the seeds and three-quarters fill the pumpkin with alternate layers of grilled croûtons and grated Gruyère. Add salt and pepper and fill up the pumpkin with cream. Put in a hot oven for 2 hours and then put it on the table. There detach the flesh of the pumpkin with a spoon. Then stir with a ladle to mix the flesh with the soup and serve."

Well, over the years I have played around with this, but have never used a giant pumpkin of the size the great Bocuse suggests. Also, although I have found the inclusion of croutons can make the soup too thick, there have been times when simply seasoned cream and Gruyère appears too thin. However, the end result, using the latter method, is quite delicious when scoops of softened pumpkin flesh are stirred into its stringy curds. Whether one should call it a soup, or a "baked pumpkin with cheese and cream," is debatable; a recipe to play with, I feel. Either way, *bonne chance!* as Chef might say . . . This is my humble, adapted effort.

1 small pumpkin, about 4 to 4½ pounds

1¾ cups heavy cream

1 garlic clove, peeled and chopped

salt and freshly ground pepper

1¼ cups freshly grated Gruyère, or Beaufort if you like

Preheat the oven to 400°F. Cut off the top quarter of the pumpkin to make a lid and set aside. Scoop out the seeds and stringy membrane using a spoon. Heat the cream with the garlic and seasoning almost to a simmer, then take off the heat, cover, and leave to infuse for 20 minutes.

Strain the infused cream into the pumpkin cavity. Mix in the cheese, put on the lid, and place in a roasting pan. Bake for 1½ to 2 hours, until the pumpkin flesh is tender when pierced with a fork and the outer skin of the pumpkin is nicely burnished; you may wish to turn the heat down slightly if the skin is becoming too brown.

Baked butternut squash with olive oil & lemon

serves 4

❖ This recipe is, of course, quite delicious in its own right: the baked squash flesh scooped from the skin into warmed, shallow bowls and dressed with lemon juice—plus a sprinkling of Parmesan if you like. The cooked flesh may also be used to make ravioli (see right).

1 butternut squash, about 2¼ pounds

salt and freshly ground pepper

3 to 4 tablespoons olive oil

lemon juice

freshly grated Parmesan, to serve (optional)

Preheat the oven to 375°F. Quarter the squash lengthwise and scoop out all seeds and stringy membrane. Place in a baking dish, season, and generously spoon olive oil over. Bake for about 1 hour, basting occasionally, until the squash is very tender when pierced with a fork. Squeeze lemon juice over to taste. Serve hot, with Parmesan, if you like.

Squash ravioli with pine nuts, butter & sage

serves 6, as a first course

❧ A hand-cranked pasta machine is fairly essential here, unless you are an adept rolling-pin pasta maker. The baked butternut squash recipe (left) should yield about 3 cups chopped (1/2-inch cubes) flesh, the quantity needed here. The recipe calls for Italian 00 flour, which is available in specialty markets. You can substitute all-purpose flour, but the results won't be as tender.

for the ravioli filling

1 onion, peeled and minced

1 tablespoon olive oil (from baking the squash, if there is some left)

2 scant tablespoons butter

3 cups chopped cooked butternut squash flesh

2 paper-wrapped amaretti cookies (4 halves), crushed

2 heaping tablespoons freshly grated Parmesan

1 large egg yolk

1 tablespoon fresh white bread crumbs

salt and freshly ground pepper

for the pasta

1¾ cups (generous) 00 pasta flour

2 large egg yolks

2 large eggs

1 teaspoon Maldon sea salt

extra beaten egg, for sealing the ravioli

to dress the pasta

large piece of butter

handful of sage leaves

handful of pine nuts

freshly grated Parmesan

To make the ravioli filling, fry the onion in the olive oil until golden and soft. Tip into a food processor and add the remaining filling ingredients. Process until fairly smooth, but not to a complete paste. Scoop out into a bowl, cover with plastic wrap, and set aside.

For the pasta, mix the ingredients together in a bowl until a firm dough is achieved (an electric food mixer with a paddle attachment, or dough hook, makes the task immeasurably easier). Knead for several minutes, wrap in plastic wrap, and allow to rest in the refrigerator for at least 30 minutes.

Take about one-sixth of the pasta and start to feed it between the rollers of the pasta machine. Take the dough up to a medium-thickness level to begin with, then fold it over like a business letter, turn it through 45° and then return to the first level. Try to do this three times; I believe this repetition gives a more supple pasta, which is more tender and giving once cooked. Take the pasta up to its thinnest level, lay out the sheet on a floured surface, and leave it to settle for a minute or two.

Now, place small teaspoonfuls of the squash mixture along the top half of the pasta sheet at, say, 2½-inch intervals. Lightly brush the pasta with egg in between the little mounds of filling and along the top edge of the sheet. Cut through from top to bottom between the filling mounds, making rectangles. To form the ravioli, fold the lower part of each rectangle onto the upper part, enclosing the blob of filling. Seal carefully using your fingertips, taking care not to trap air inside. Repeat with the rest of the pasta and filling, to make about 30 large ravioli in total.

To cook the ravioli, add it to a pan of boiling salted water and boil gently for 4 to 5 minutes, or until tender. Lift one out to check it is cooked; when pinched with the fingers the edges should easily give to the touch.

Meanwhile, for the dressing, melt the butter in a small skillet and add the sage leaves and pine nuts. Cook slowly, stirring occasionally, until the sage leaves become crisp and the pine nuts are golden. Drain the ravioli and divide among warmed bowls. Spoon the warm dressing over and sprinkle with Parmesan.

Cabbage & Chard

I was not a difficult child when it came to eating my greens. In fact, I can remember only one occasion when something Mum cooked that I did not like reappeared for supper. Mind you, it can't have been that terrible, as I now cannot for the life of me recall what it was. But greens it would never have been.

I always adored servings of soft and buttery, well-peppered cabbage. The varieties we ate—and those that I prefer to this day—are either the light green and pointy cabbage ("hispi," I think, is the name of this variety) or the firmer, paler and sort of round-toward-oval shaped cabbage, which is nowhere near as huge and hard as the big brute—sometimes called Dutch—that is used for making coleslaw. Our cabbage was properly cooked, too.

Cabbage should be trimmed and cut—including the core—into either quarters or sixths, if large. Boil in generously salted water until just tender, then drain. Lay the cabbage on a dish towel and allow to cool a little. Now place on a cutting board, cut away the core, and slice the leaves into large pieces. Return to the pan, add as much butter and pepper as you dare, then gently reheat and allow to very gently stew for 4 to 5 minutes, stirring occasionally. I hope you will agree with me that the result is supremely fine, hot buttered cabbage.

Of Savoy, the dark green crinkled one, I have never been much of a fan. There is something slightly bitter within, together with a slight, sulfurous quality that displeases me. I know that many will not agree—one of them, in particular, being my colleague and friend Rowley Leigh, with whom such disagreements are frequent, but always good-natured and stimulating.

I know hardly anything at all about cavolo nero, the more recent darling of the newer, rustic kitchen (a contradiction in terms, but undeniably apt). I have never cooked this long and deeply dark green leafed Italian cabbage, but thoroughly enjoyed its almost stygian strands within its happiest home: a deep bowlful of *ribollita*, the "reboiled" gorgeous thick soup so beloved of all Tuscans. That which is served at The River Café, in West London, is one of the finest I have eaten.

Chard—or Swiss chard, to give it its full name—is a most useful and interesting plant, cookery wise, as it offers the opportunity to make two completely different dishes from the one vegetable. The glossy and deeply veined dark green leaves may be trimmed away from the fleshy stalks (sharp scissors are good here). The leaves are best coarsely shredded and cooked simply in butter or olive oil. The stalks are at their finest, I think, when washed, trimmed, and cut into short lengths, then steamed or boiled, laid in a shallow dish, and covered with a light cheese sauce and baked as a gratin. Delicious. Please do try the recipe (on page 48).

Finally, Korean kimchi (on page 46) is not for the fainthearted, but it is undeniably good for those who—how shall we say?—enjoy their food particularly perky—and also have the patience to wait. Read on . . .

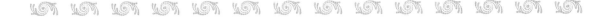

Korean kimchi

makes about 1 quart

◈ This is adapted from a recipe in *Foods from the Far East*, by Bruce Cost, first published in the United States about twenty years ago. One of my favorite cookery books, it should be essential reading for all those interested in cooking with Asian ingredients. Bruce's far-reaching Asian menu at Monsoon, his restaurant in San Francisco, was diverse—the kitchen producing remarkable dishes of great delicacy, yet with a heat, spice, and freshness that made them unique.

Try to find a room in your home that you don't mind becoming quite smelly during the making of kimchi! The fermentation period (the smelly period) should not be done out of doors unless, I guess, if it is warm weather. I once tried doing this outside in winter and the process slowed right down to almost nothing. Under the stairs might be better, perhaps?

In Korea, kimchi is eaten every single day, particularly at breakfast time, I understand.

2 small napa (Chinese) cabbages, about 1¾ pounds in total

3 teaspoons Maldon sea salt

2 scallions, trimmed and cut into short lengths

¼ cup (scant) peeled and roughly chopped fresh ginger

6 or 7 large garlic cloves, peeled and roughly chopped

2 teaspoons dried red chili flakes

4 large fresh red chilis, seeded

2 teaspoons sugar

Slice the cabbage crosswise at 1½-inch intervals and toss with the salt in a very large bowl or stainless steel pan. Barely cover with cold water and mix together with your hands to disperse the salt. Leave to soak overnight in the kitchen (this is not the smelly part).

The next day, drain the leaves in a colander, but do not rinse. Return to the wiped-out bowl or pan, add the scallions, and mix together. Put the ginger, garlic, chili flakes, fresh chilis, and sugar into a small food processor and grind to a not-too-fine paste. Add this to the leaves and scallions and mix together well with a spatula or wooden spoon; you might think hands are best here, but believe me, they are not (think culinary Lady Macbeth).

Now pack into a preserving jar that will generously accommodate the cabbage and seal. Allow to mature and ferment at room temperature over a period of 4 to 5 days. Two or three times each day, open the lid to allow gas to escape (the smell), running a chopstick down the inside of the glass to further facilitate this. Although you may think during this period that the mixture smells far too strong, it will mellow and soften, be assured.

Once the kimchi is ready, store it in the refrigerator, where it will keep for several weeks. I think it is particularly delicious eaten with simply steamed rice, but I can nibble on it at any time. A very healthful food.

Cabbage, caraway & pepper soup with potato dumplings

serves 4

❖ You may like to further enhance this nourishing soup by sprinkling a little crumbled Roquefort or other good-quality blue cheese over each serving.

The recipe for the dumplings will make more than you need. I suggest you keep the extra mixture until the following day, to enjoy the dumplings in their own right—boiled and dressed either with some fonduta (see page 179) or a little hot butter, in which sage leaves have been crisped, and a dusting of freshly grated Parmesan.

for the dumplings

¾ to 1 pound waxy potatoes, peeled

3 scant tablespoons butter

1 large egg

⅓ cup self-rising flour

½ teaspoon baking powder

1 teaspoon Maldon sea salt

for the soup

2 scant tablespoons butter

a small glug of olive oil

1 leek, trimmed, well washed, and thinly sliced

1 large onion, peeled and minced

1 large carrot, peeled and grated

4 large garlic cloves, peeled and minced

5 cups stock

1 teaspoon caraway seeds

2 teaspoons freshly ground black pepper, not too fine

salt

5 cups shredded, then coarsely chopped, green cabbage

1 heaping tablespoon chopped parsley

For the dumplings, put the potatoes into a steamer and cook until very tender. Allow them to dry out for a few minutes and, while still hot, pass through a potato ricer (best) or a food mill into a bowl, but try not to overwork them. Now, thoroughly beat in the remaining ingredients and leave to cool and firm up in the refrigerator.

For the soup, heat the butter and olive oil in another large pan, add the leek, onion, carrot, and garlic and fry gently until softened but not colored. Add the stock, caraway, pepper, and salt to taste. Bring up to a simmer and cook for 20 minutes. Meanwhile, bring a large pan of salted water to a gentle boil for the dumplings.

Add the cabbage to the soup and continue to simmer until it is tender. To cook the dumplings, scoop up little balls of potato mixture with an oiled teaspoon and drop them into the boiling water; five per person is about right. They will swell slightly, float up to the surface, and be ready in 4 to 5 minutes.

To assemble, stir the parsley into the simmering soup, decant into four hot soup bowls, and add the dumplings. Serve directly.

Chard leaves with ramps & olive oil

serves 2

❖ This recipe deals with the leaves; the one below uses the equally delicious stalks. They may happily be served as separate dishes, although offering them together could present a most appealing contrast of texture and flavor and make a complete meal for two.

chard leaves, cut from a
1-pound bunch (stalks
saved for the following
recipe), washed

2 handfuls ramps, washed
and trimmed

2 tablespoons olive oil

salt and freshly ground
pepper

Slice the chard leaves and ramps into wide ribbons. Heat the olive oil in a large skillet and add the leaves and seasoning. Gently fry, stirring all together well, until beginning to wilt and then allow to stew until soft and tender. About 15 to 20 minutes all told. Serve piping hot.

Chard au gratin

serves 2

❖ Cheese-blistered stalks, presented *au gratin*, are most attractive to look at, particularly when they are served alongside a bowl of glossy, dark chard leaves and ramps.

2 tablespoons butter

2 teaspoons all-purpose
flour

1 cup (scant) milk

¼ cup freshly grated
Gruyère

⅓ cup freshly grated
Parmesan

salt, freshly ground white
pepper, and a scraping of
nutmeg

chard stalks saved from
1-pound bunch in above
recipe

Preheat the oven to 400°F. To make the sauce (Mornay, in fact), melt the butter in a saucepan and stir in the flour. Cook gently for a few minutes, then pour in the milk all at once and whisk together thoroughly. Place the pan over low heat and stir constantly until the sauce begins to thicken; any lumps that form will eventually disappear (this method has always worked for me).

Add the Gruyère, a little over half of the Parmesan, and the seasonings. Allow to simmer very gently indeed (a heat-diffuser mat is useful), stirring occasionally, for about 15 to 20 minutes; this slow cooking makes for a good sauce Mornay—I use it for all béchamel-based sauces.

Meanwhile, peel the chard stalks with a vegetable peeler and cut into 4-inch lengths. Steam (or boil) until tender, about 20 minutes, then remove and lay on paper towels or a dish towel to dry.

Lightly butter a gratin dish and lay the chard stalks in it. Pour the sauce over and sprinkle with the remaining Parmesan. Bake in the oven for about 20 minutes, or until nicely golden and bubbling.

Carrots & Parsnips

When our restaurant Bibendum opened its doors, twenty-two years ago now, so pedantically keen was I to do the right thing that we cooked our *carottes Vichy* in bottles of very expensive Vichy water; well, "very expensive" is relative, but, when several bottles were being used each day just to cook vegetables, the cost began to mount up . . .

But they were delicious, those carrots, even if their association with Vichy had nothing whatever to do with its mineral water. I guess that the slightly saline, very slightly sweet flavor of Vichy water made them taste so perfectly seasoned. Incidentally, I love to drink Vichy water, too, and it is especially effective when suffering with tummy troubles—it beats Dioralyte any day.

I think certain organic vegetables taste better than others—onions, for instance, some potato varieties, and parsnips, too. Big bunches of British blanched winter celery, usually organic, have a particularly wonderful flavor. But, you know, I always see a carrot as, well, just that . . . a carrot. I realize I shall be shouted down and beaten with a stick in some quarters, but I remain steadfast in this belief. It is what one does to a carrot in the kitchen that makes it taste so much better.

About a year ago, friends in Kent (who have a very big garden indeed) presented me with freshly dug parsnips for Sunday lunch. Even their raw scent pervaded the kitchen. The immediacy from earth to table obviously helped hugely, but the intense flavor was just marvelous. Then again, perhaps this was not unusual, as I had never previously eaten freshly dug, home-grown parsnips. Anyway, I simply boiled them and made a purée with much butter and a touch of cream. Jane and Robert still talk of that purée, but you could have boiled them in old bathwater and still they would have tasted good, such was their provenance and almost overpowering freshness. One day, of course, they will further shock me with their carrots . . .

To make a fine purée, it is best to steam the parsnips, first cut up into small chunks. Once tender, they should preferably be worked through the finest disk of a food mill. Then it is simply a case of beating in as much butter and cream as seems, at least, sensible, together with salt and plenty of freshly ground white pepper. A spoonful of smooth Dijon mustard whisked in at the very last minute is quite nice, too. Once heated too much, mustard loses its punch, so it is better as a late addition.

Kay Henderson's carrot timbale

serves 4

❖ Kay Henderson, together with her husband, Paul, opened the wonderful Gidleigh Park Hotel on the edge of Dartmoor, Devon, in 1977. This charming little first course was one of the very earliest dishes on the menu when Kay herself was in the kitchen. The following recipe is my adaptation to suit this book, but thanks must go to Kay for inspiring the idea in the first place, even though Paul thinks it initially came via the legendary Michel Guérard. Although Paul and Kay sold the hotel in 2005, they continue to live close by, so much do they adore their Devon idyll.

To give the timbale a pleasing, faintly nubby texture once cooked, I would recommend first chopping the carrot and onion into small chunks, then pulsing them in a food processor until the texture of coarse sea salt. Together with the melting strands of cheese—and faint anise flavor from the chervil—this will produce the most delicate little dish.

3 tablespoons butter, plus a little extra (softened) for greasing the molds

¾ to 1 pound carrots, peeled and finely minced

1 medium onion, peeled and finely minced

large pinch of sugar

salt and freshly ground pepper

1¼ cups stock

2 large eggs

½ cup grated Gruyère or, even better, Beaufort (if you can find it)

2 tablespoons heavy cream

2 tablespoons minced chervil leaves

for the sauce

1 tablespoon sherry vinegar

1 tablespoon dry vermouth

2 tablespoons cold butter, cut into small chunks

squeeze of lemon juice (optional)

Preheat the oven to 300°F. Generously butter four ramekins and line the base of each with a tiny disk of waxed paper.

Using a nonstick skillet, for preference, melt the butter and gently fry the carrots and onion with the sugar, a little salt, and a generous grinding of pepper until beginning to burnish lightly. Add the stock and allow the mixture to simmer until the carrots are fully cooked and the liquid has reduced by about half.

Place a coarse strainer over a bowl and strain the carrot mixture, stirring it around in the sieve for a moment, but then allowing the liquid to drip through naturally for 10 minutes or so, rather than forcing it. The strained liquid should measure approximately ⅔ cup. Pour it into a small saucepan and set to one side. Tip the carrot pulp into the empty bowl, add the eggs, Gruyère, cream, and chervil, and mix well. Check for seasoning.

Pour the carrot mixture into the prepared ramekins, filling them to the brim. Cover each with a circle of foil and place in a deep baking dish. Pour tap-hot water into the dish until it comes at least three-quarters of the way up the sides of the ramekins. Bake in the oven for 20 to 25 minutes, or until firm to the touch.

To make the sauce, add the vinegar and vermouth to the carrot liquid and reduce it again, by about half. Remove from the heat and whisk in the cold butter, a piece at a time, until the sauce is glossy and richly flavored. Sharpen with lemon juice only if you wish to.

Once the timbales are cooked, carefully turn out from their ramekins onto warmed plates—not forgetting to remove the little disk of waxed paper. Coat with a little of the sauce and serve at once.

Carrot salad with cilantro & green chili

serves 4

❈ A nice fall dish that is delicious in itself, but also very good eaten alongside the garlic, saffron & tomato quiche (see page 88). Fresh, zingy, and magnificently inexpensive.

4 cups peeled and finely grated carrots

1 ½ teaspoons Maldon sea salt

1 ½ teaspoons superfine sugar

juice of 1 small lime

1 teaspoon coriander seeds

cilantro leaves picked from 4 or 5 bushy sprigs

1 large green chili, seeded

In a large bowl, mix the grated carrot together with the salt, sugar, and lime juice. Leave to macerate for at least 30 minutes.

Meanwhile, place the coriander seeds in a small, dry skillet and gently toast them over low heat until they smell very good, but be careful not to burn them. Tip into a mortar and lightly crush with the pestle.

Now mince the cilantro and chili together (this makes for a more aromatic mix, in a similar way to *persillade*—garlic and parsley given the same treatment). Add to the carrots together with the coriander seeds and mix well. Turn into a serving dish.

Parsnip soup with masala cream

serves 4

✦ This is the time to make a batch of Indian masala paste (see right). Of course, parsnip soup has always had an affinity with curry, for which I would say, we have the estimable British cookery writer, Jane Grigson to thank.

3 tablespoons butter

1 large leek, trimmed, washed, and sliced

1 pound parsnips, peeled and diced

⅓ cup (scant) dry sherry

3 cups stock

salt

for the masala cream

¾ cup heavy cream

2 to 3 teaspoons masala paste, to taste

Melt the butter in a roomy pot and gently sweat the leek until soft. Add the parsnips and cook, covered, over very low heat, for another 5 minutes or so. Remove the lid, turn up the heat, and pour in the sherry. Bubble hard for a few minutes until most of the liquid has been driven off, then add the stock. Season with salt to taste and bring up to a low simmer. Cover once more and cook until the parsnips are very soft, about 25 minutes.

Meanwhile, for the masala cream, pour the cream into a small saucepan and whisk in the masala paste. Warm through, cover, and leave to infuse.

Once the parsnips are cooked, tip the soup into a blender, process until smooth, and then pass through a fine strainer into a clean pan. (By the way, I like my creamed soups to be *really* smooth and silky.) Reheat gently, adding a little more stock or water if the soup is too thick.

Ladle into warmed bowls and spoon some of the masala cream on top of each serving, allowing each person to stir it in to flavor the soup.

Masala paste

makes about 3 cups

◇ This paste is ever so useful for all sorts of vegetable, legume, and rice preparations when a complex whiff of Asian spice is called for. I find it to be a most practical commodity kept at the back of the refrigerator in a sealed jar, and further kept in good shape by a film of oil over the surface. When some of the paste is used, simply smooth over the surface and add a tiny bit more oil to cover.

4 tablespoons cumin seeds

2 tablespoons coriander seeds

2 teaspoons fennel seeds

2 teaspoons brown mustard seeds

2 teaspoons whole cloves

2 teaspoons small, dried red chilis, or a little more if you like it hot

small handful of curry leaves, slightly less if dried (optional)

10 ounces onions, peeled and chopped

22 to 25 garlic cloves, peeled and chopped

²⁄₃ cup (scant) peeled and chopped fresh ginger

2 tablespoons tamarind paste

2 teaspoons turmeric

2 tablespoons red wine vinegar

¼ cup unsweetened shredded coconut

¼ cup coconut milk

2 teaspoons Maldon sea salt

2 teaspoons superfine sugar

Using a nonstick skillet, lightly toast the whole spices: cumin, coriander, fennel, and mustard seeds, cloves and chilis, until smelling quite wonderful and pungent, but be careful not to burn them. Tip into a small bowl to cool. Once the spices are cool, process them in a coffee grinder, or similar, until powdered.

Place the curry leaves (if using), onions, garlic, ginger, tamarind paste, turmeric, vinegar, shredded coconut, coconut milk, salt, and sugar in a food processor. Add the freshly ground spices and process everything until as smooth as possible; this will depend on the sharpness of your blade and the power of the machine. (Do not be tempted to add the spices whole, as they will remain "bitty" if not previously powdered.)

There is enough here to fill 2 small preserving jars of 1½-cup capacity. Cover with a film of oil and refrigerate until needed.

Cheese-crusted fried parsnip strips with romesco sauce

serves 2

❖ Perfect as a wintry Sunday night television supper snack, eaten in front of the fire with fingers and napkins. The quantities for the romesco will probably make more than you need, but it keeps well in the refrigerator for several days and is delicious spread onto toasted baguette. Although the ingredients here are mostly from store-bought jars, the end result is very good. If there is enough, I use the oil in which the tomatoes have been immersed for the olive oil in the recipe.

¾ pound parsnips, peeled

⅔ cup white bread crumbs made from semistale bread

⅔ cup freshly grated Parmesan

¼ teaspoon cayenne pepper

salt

1 large egg, beaten

flour for coating

oil for deep- or shallow-frying (a neutral-flavored oil, such as sunflower or peanut)

for the romesco sauce

⅓ cup (heaping) skinned almonds

4 tablespoons olive oil

1 large garlic clove, peeled and chopped

1 small dried chili

½ cup (rounded) oven-dried tomatoes from a jar, drained

½ cup (rounded) piquillo peppers from a jar, drained

1 tablespoon sherry vinegar

1 tablespoon hot water

salt

For the romesco sauce, gently fry the almonds in 1 teaspoon of the olive oil until golden. Allow to cool, then tip them into a food processor and add the garlic, chili, tomatoes, peppers, vinegar, and hot water. Grind to a nubby purée and then add salt to taste. Adjust the quantity of vinegar, if you wish for a sharper flavor.

Cut the parsnips into broad strips, about 2½ inches long, and steam until only just tender, then set aside on a plate to cool.

Mix the bread crumbs with the cheese, cayenne, and salt in a shallow dish. Have the beaten egg ready in a similar dish, and the flour in another one. To coat the parsnips, first dip the strips in flour, then in the egg, and, finally, in the bread crumb and cheese mixture.

To fry the parsnip strips, either use a deep-fat fryer or a deep skillet containing a ¾-inch depth of oil. Heat the oil to 325°F in the deep-fryer or, if using the skillet method, until a small cube of bread turns golden in a minute or so.

Fry the parsnips in the hot oil in batches until crisp and golden, then briefly drain on paper towels. Serve at once, with the sauce alongside.

Peas & Beans

My friend Sarah de Teliga, who is Australian, but has lived off and on in Paris for a number of years, recently related to me a both sweet and sad little *histoire* regarding a French friend of her son, Linus. They were probably about ten or eleven years old at the time, Sarah thinks, and Linus had invited his friend home for supper one early summer evening, after school. Sarah had roasted a delicious chicken, perhaps, and accompanied it with some peak-of-the-season *haricots verts très fins*—in other words, very fine French beans that are the width of pipe cleaners.

All seemed to be going well, although the boy appeared to be a bit shy, Sarah thought. It was not until she noticed a trickle of tears rolling down his increasingly pink cheeks, that she realized there was a more underlying problem than simply shyness: the boy was clearly troubled by something. Sarah discreetly inquired as to what the problem might be by nudging Linus, but was met with a (recently learned, no doubt) Gallic shrug. Then she asked the poor boy what his dilemma might be, by which time he was convulsed by full-blown blubbing.

Well, it transpired that he had grave concerns over the fact that Sarah's *haricots verts* had not been both "topped and tailed," as we British say; although the stem ends had been trimmed ("topped"), the other, spiky, end (the "tail") had not. There followed a clear qualification for his distress, that his mother would never have countenanced such a lamentable *faux pas*. Quite simply, the boy was not going to eat them. Sarah then asked him what he would like to do. He said, most emphatically, that he would be going home now. So home he went.

Whether the boy was ever invited back for supper and, if he was, Sarah had tried to be more diligent with her beans, I have never inquired. But, much as I adore Sarah, who loves to cook and has a notable affinity with good food (her younger son, Nestor, tells me that Sarah's version of *my* rice pudding recipe is better than mine), I am with the boy on this one—though, perhaps, with a little more *politesse* and tantrum-free.

Not to tail a French bean is never considered by French cooks. The very idea is inconceivable. I just hope that what I believe started as a lazy British habit—and first noted by me around about the mid-1980s—does not travel across the Channel. They get stuck in your teeth, those nasty little spikes and, therefore, utterly spoil the pleasure of eating such bundles of sweet tenderness at each and every mouthful. For me, this heretical behavior is as bad as serving boiled potatoes with their skins remaining attached.

I wonder how impressed the fastidious French boy would have been with the dish of fresh peas I was once served in the top floor restaurant of the London Hilton: every single pea had been *individually peeled*!

Now, I know I can often be accused of an (impeccably) mannered approach to certain cookery practices (see above), but even I have never been tempted to peel peas. However, it must here be said that these peas were indeed impeccable and absolutely delicious; so green and tender, and further finished with good butter. Each pea had naturally split in half as dried "split" peas do. Fear not, however; I shall not be including a recipe in which I ask you to "Hilton" your peas.

Petits pois à la française

serves 4

◇ Clearly, the finest peas for this classy and lovely French dish would be ones that you have freshly picked and shelled—either homegrown or collected from a pick-your-own farm. If not, there is little point in using shelled peas from, say, a supermarket. Tempting and labor-free though these might seem, they can often be worthless in terms of taste and texture, as any fresh sweetness they may have once had will have turned to starch. If in doubt, I would always suggest frozen—and the more *petit*, the better. The mint is very un-French, but I like it here.

7 tablespoons (1 scant stick) butter, softened

1 large romaine lettuce

6 scallions, white part only, thickly sliced

3½ cups frozen peas

salt and freshly ground white pepper

several mint leaves, chopped

Preheat the oven to 310°F. Bring a pan of salted water to a boil. Take a lidded, shallow ovenproof pan and thickly smear the inside—both bottom and sides—with about one-third of the butter. Separate about 10 to 12 large, outer dark green leaves from the lettuce (depending on the size of your pan) and briefly blanch in the boiling water until just beginning to flop. Plunge into iced water and lay out to dry on a dish towel.

Carefully and neatly lay the blanched lettuce leaves in the pan, placing the core ends in the middle, with the rounded ends of the leaves creeping up the sides, overlapping them slightly and pressing them onto the butter so that they stick. The end result should look like a large, green flower. Reserve a couple of leaves for the top.

Cut the remaining lettuce—the heart—across into shreds and put into a bowl. Add the scallions, peas, seasoning, mint, and another one-third of the butter, in flecks. Mix together and carefully tip into the lettuce-lined pan. Press down lightly and lay the reserved leaves on top. Now bring the edges of the lining leaves over the top to form a kind of "lettuce lid." Melt the remainder of the butter and spoon over the surface.

Cut a waxed paper circle slightly bigger than the diameter of the pan, dampen it, and then lightly press it down onto the lettuce surface and against the sides of the pan. This "cartouche" helps to ensure that as much moisture as possible remains within the pea stew as it cooks. There should be no need to add any extra liquid.

Finally, place the lid on the pan and slide it into the oven. Cook for about 1 hour. A good sign that it is ready is when the lettuce and peas have become a dull green color and are very soft indeed. In fact, for me, the end result should almost be redolent of the best-quality canned peas!

Fine beans in a cream vinaigrette with shallots

serves 4

❖ Use the very finest green beans you can find for this recipe.

1 pound thin green beans, trimmed

salt and freshly ground pepper

1 level tablespoon good-quality Dijon mustard

1 tablespoon white wine or tarragon vinegar

2 shallots, peeled and minced

$\frac{2}{3}$ cup whipping cream

generous sprinkling of chopped parsley

Add the beans to a pan of fiercely boiling salted water and cook briskly until just tender, but not "squeaky" to the bite. Drain and refresh in iced water to stop the cooking and set the color. Drain once more and lay on a clean dish towel to dry thoroughly.

In a bowl, whisk together the mustard, vinegar, and some seasoning. Add the shallots and whisk in the cream. Taste the vinaigrette for seasoning.

Arrange the beans in a serving dish, spoon the dressing over, and sprinkle generously with chopped parsley to serve.

A small stew of fava beans with summer savory

serves 2

✤ Summer savory has always been seen as a fine partner to fava beans. Although not an herb readily available in the supermarkets, it may be found in pots at garden centers, or, of course, you could grow your own from seed. Lemon thyme and tarragon are other possibilities for this stew.

3 pounds fava beans, shelled

salt and freshly ground white pepper

3 scant tablespoons butter

1 small onion (preferably white), peeled and minced

1 cup whipping cream

2 teaspoons chopped summer savory leaves (or lemon thyme or tarragon)

squeeze of lemon juice

Add the fava beans to a pan of boiling salted water and boil for 2 to 3 minutes only. Drain.

Melt the butter in a pan, add the onion, and stew for a few moments until softened. Now tip in the beans and turn them around in the buttery onions for a few seconds, then pour in the cream. Bring up to a boil and simmer until the liquid has thickened and the beans are tender.

Stir in the savory and lemon juice and serve without delay. Very delicious spooned over a slice of bruschetta.

Pea & potato samosas

makes about 40 small samosas

❖ These samosas do not use traditional Indian pastry, but the filling tastes—to me, at least—authentic and good. You will need a quantity of both green paste and masala paste. However, once these are made, the assembly of the samosas takes very little time, especially as the "pastry" I have chosen to use is from a package of Asian spring roll wrappers. I have also come across frozen packs of samosa pastry in supermarkets, complete with folding directions on the back of the package.

It is important to keep the wrappers moist while working with them. Have a damp dish towel on hand to keep the remainder covered as you work with each one.

1½ pounds waxy potatoes, washed

2 tablespoons oil or ghee

1 onion, peeled and minced

1½ tablespoons masala paste (see page 55)

1¾ cups cooked peas

1 tablespoon green paste (see page 157)

salt

juice of ½ lemon

1 heaping tablespoon chopped cilantro leaves

20 sheets spring roll wrappers, 6 inches square

1 large egg, beaten

oil for shallow- or deep-frying

Steam (preferably) or boil the potatoes in their skins until tender. Drain and cool, then peel and cut into chunks. Heat the oil or ghee in a pan and gently fry the onion until golden brown. Add the masala paste and stir around for a minute or two to cook the spices. Remove from the heat, tip in the peas and potatoes, and mix well. Now stir in the green paste and a little salt, breaking up the vegetables somewhat at the same time. Sharpen the mixture with lemon juice and mix in the chopped cilantro. Tip into a bowl and allow to cool completely.

To form each samosa, cut a wrapper in half, to give two rectangles. Take one of these and place a teaspoonful of the pea and potato mix at one end. Brush the edges with egg and then fold one-third of the rectangle over the filling into a triangle shape. Now fold this one-third over again, but in the opposite direction. Finally, fold this over onto the final one-third to form a completed, triangular package. Squeeze the edges together with your fingers to form a tight seal and move on to the next one. Set the completed samosas aside on a tray or plate; it does not matter one jot, now, if they begin to dry out a little.

To cook the samosas, heat a ¾ to 1-inch depth of oil in a skillet (or use a deep-fryer) over medium heat until it reaches 325°F. To check the oil is hot enough, drop in a cube of bread; it should turn golden within a minute or so. Fry 4 or 5 samosas at a time, being careful not to overcrowd the pan. Fry gently, turning the samosas frequently until they are crisp and golden. (I sometimes transfer them to a flat tray in a medium oven, to both keep hot and become more golden and crisp, turning them occasionally.) Drain on paper towels and serve hot.

A good, instant dip can be made by mixing plain yogurt with lots of chopped mint, a little chopped green chili, a pinch each of sugar and salt, and a squeeze of lime juice. I also find some mango chutney is another, essential condiment.

Leeks & Onions

There was a time when the lovely leek was simply not available for purchase during the summer months. Or, if there were some late spring stragglers, their centers—often making up about two-thirds of the vegetable—would be nothing but impenetrable woody sticks. Not so now, with perfect leeks being available all year round —and in perfect condition.

I do not necessarily agree with all out-of-season imports; Peruvian asparagus appearing on the shelves when homegrown spears that I cut myself have been available for at least two weeks, is one particular irritation. However, I must admit, the leek situation suits me perfectly, as it allows me to enjoy my favorite cold leek and potato soup, the dreamily delicious vichyssoise, all summer long.

I adore this pale, pale soup, just with the merest hint of background green to its cool and creamy appearance. In fact, I have often wondered whether there has ever been a house paint named after vichyssoise, so pretty would it look in a bathroom or sunny kitchen. Anyway, interior design aside, another important aspect of the soup should be its consistency: limpid and not at all thick. It should pour easily when served and be almost as thin as the consistency of whipping cream, which, I would suggest is the cream to employ when making vichyssoise, rather than an overly rich heavy cream.

All cold soups, including vichyssoise, should be thoroughly chilled for maximum enjoyment; otherwise they are neither one thing nor the other. I have often debated with fellow cooks as to whether one should use butter when stewing the leeks at the initial stages of making vichyssoise. After all, once chilled, the butter content, however well homogenized in the blending thereof, will remain as minute, chilled butter flecks. I have tried using no fat whatsoever, simply simmering the leeks and potatoes together in well seasoned stock, before blending in the cream, but I don't think it has quite enough flavor and has a bit of a "boiled" taste to it.

I now admit to having had the best success with one of those "spreadable butters" (awful name, I know), which are made by blending butter with a neutral oil. Once the sliced leeks—and almost all white parts, please—have cooked to a semisoft consistency, add roughly the same quantity of small pieces of chopped, peeled potatoes (a variety that you can trust to break up easily), and stew both vegetables together until softened. Cover generously with half stock and half milk, simmer until the potatoes are collapsing and then liquidize until super-smooth. Pass through a fine strainer, stir in some whipping cream, and chill. Serve in ice-cold soup bowls and scatter a generous amount of chopped chives on top.

Onions are equally delicious when given the same treatment, but as a hot soup. So, butter is fine now, and good stock, but without other dairy additions. Minced parsley is the herb to stir in at the end, together with plenty of freshly ground white pepper.

Onion & blood orange salad with olive oil

serves 2

◈ Does not this recipe qualify as one of the most simple and delicious in this book? Well, delicious in anyone's book, come to that. The secret, of course, *is* its simplicity, together with the sheer beauty of the thing, once carefully assembled. And I do urge you to make the most of your knife skills when slicing both oranges and onions; do as thin as you dare! Also, this is one moment in one's culinary life where extra cash should be expended on the extra-virgin oil.

Some recipes I have come across for this Sicilian specialty ask that black olives be included in the dish. Traditional it may be, but I urge you to resist. Also, I prefer sweet white onions, as opposed to the possibly more usual red ones. *Pace!*

4 blood oranges	Cut the tops and bottoms off the oranges and, using a small, very sharp knife, slice off the skins of the oranges, cutting close to the flesh and removing all traces of pith. Slice thinly (removing any seeds) and arrange neatly, slightly overlapping, on a beautiful plate.
1 or 2 small, sweet white onions, peeled	
extra-virgin olive oil	
freshly ground black pepper	Thinly slice the onions and lay them on top of the oranges. Spoon enough olive oil onto the assembly to suit you, and then grind some pepper over. Eat all by itself, and with someone you like very much.

Asian leeks "vinaigrette" with salted duck egg

serves 2

❖ Salted duck eggs are available from Asian grocery stores and, in my opinion, are quite delicious. Do not, however, confuse them with "thousand-year-old eggs," which are an acquired taste, to be sure. Simply hard-boil some fresh duck eggs if salted ones are unavailable.

4 medium leeks, trimmed of almost all green parts, or 8 smaller ones

for the vinaigrette

2 tablespoons light soy sauce

1 tablespoon sesame oil

1 to 2 tablespoons sunflower oil, or other neutral oil

2 teaspoons hoisin or plum sauce

1 tablespoon lemon juice

1 garlic clove, crushed and finely minced

to garnish

1 salted (or freshly hard–boiled) duck egg, grated

a little sliced green chili (optional)

1 teaspoon very finely sliced scallion tops

several cilantro leaves

If using medium leeks, slice them into 1-inch lengths; if using small ones, leave them whole. Either way, wash the leeks very thoroughly.

To make the vinaigrette, simply whisk the ingredients together in a small bowl until well amalgamated. Leave to infuse.

Boil the leeks in lightly salted water until tender (or steam them if you like). Lift them out carefully with a slotted spoon and put to drain and cool on a dish towel.

Arrange the cooled leeks in a suitable dish and spoon the dressing over. Sprinkle the egg and chili (if using) on top, together with the scallion and cilantro. Eat as is, or with some plain boiled rice.

Leek & cheese pie

serves 4

❖ This recipe is based on a cheese and onion pie made by my mother and particularly adored by my brother and I when we were growing up.

for the pie crust

8 tablespoons (1 stick) butter

1½ cups (scant) self-rising flour

pinch of salt

ice-cold water, to mix

for the filling

2 tablespoons butter

3 large leeks, white part only, thinly sliced

1 cup water

salt and freshly ground white pepper

10 ounces sharp Cheddar, grated

a little milk, to both seal and glaze the pie crust

To make the pie crust, cut the butter into small chunks and place in a large bowl with the flour and salt. Gently rub the fat into the flour, using fingertips, until the texture resembles very coarse bread crumbs. Mix in enough water to just bind the mixture together as a dough without it becoming too slack and wet; in other words, be cautious with the water. Knead the dough until fully amalgamated, dust with flour, and slip into a plastic bag. Place in the refrigerator to rest for 30 minutes before using.

Preheat the oven to 350°F and also place a flat baking sheet in there, too, which will help to cook the base of the pie more evenly.

Meanwhile, prepare the filling. Melt the butter in a roomy pan, add the leeks, and allow to quietly wilt and stew for 10 minutes over gentle heat without coloring. Now tip in the water, salt, and plenty of pepper. Continue to cook over similar heat, stirring occasionally, until almost all liquid has been driven off. Decant the leeks onto a plate, spread them out and allow to cool.

Lightly butter an 8-inch loose-bottomed tart pan, 1½ inches deep. On a lightly floured counter, roll out two-thirds of the pie crust moderately thinly and use to line the pan. Now roll out the remainder to a round of similar thickness, large enough to use as a lid to the pie. Cover the base of the pie with half of the cooked leeks and then cover with half the grated cheese. Repeat these layers.

Brush the edges of the pie crust with milk. Position the pie crust lid and press the edges together lightly to seal, then trim off any excess overhang. Brush the surface of the pie with milk. Make three small incisions in the middle of the pie, using the point of a sharp knife, and, if you wish, decorate the edge with light indentations from the tines of a fork.

Place the pan on the hot baking sheet and bake the pie on the middle shelf of the oven for 40 to 50 minutes, or until it is pale golden and tiny oozes of cheesy-leeky juices are bubbling up through the holes in the middle of the pie. Remove from the oven and leave for 20 minutes before unmolding and cutting into generous wedges. Best served warm, and is extremely good with piccalilli, too.

Boiled onions with poached egg & Lancashire cheese

serves 4

❊ I was first informed of this quite astonishingly simple bowl of goodness by a young chef who had previously worked at a well renowned Lancashire pub, The Three Fishes, in the village of Mitton. Although "boiled onions" hardly sounds enticing, it is, in fact, absolutely everything it says—and why on earth call it anything else? "Fancy names mean nowt," my grandfather would have said; and he was a Lancashire man, too, through and through.

It is imperative to use both white-skinned onions and ground white pepper here, to ensure the correct texture and traditional flavor. I have added a bay leaf, too, which is not in the original recipe; you might prefer to omit it.

1 pound white-skinned onions, peeled and coarsely but neatly diced

1½ cups water

3 tablespoons butter

scant ½ teaspoon ready-ground white pepper

2 teaspoons Maldon sea salt

1 bay leaf (optional)

splash of malt vinegar (optional)

10 ounces Lancashire or Cheddar or similar tasty cheese, coarsely grated

4 large eggs

2 tablespoons minced curly parsley

Put the onions into a pan with the water, butter, pepper, salt, and bay leaf (if using). Bring to a boil, turn down to a low simmer, cover, and cook for about 30 minutes, or until the onions are nice and soft.

Heat the broiler to medium. Have ready a pan of simmering water with a healthy splash of malt vinegar added, if desired, to poach the eggs.

Once the onions are ready, stir well and then divide between four warmed, ovenproof, shallow dishes. Now sprinkle with the cheese and place under the broiler to just melt the cheese, *not* to brown it.

Meanwhile, poach the eggs in the simmering water. Remove with a slotted spoon to drain and place one on top of each dish of onions and cheese. Sprinkle the parsley over and serve without delay.

Fennel & Celery

It was with enormous pleasure that, on two occasions, I was privileged to lunch at the table of Lulu Peyraud, at Domaine Tempier in Bandol, in the South of France. Her late husband, Lucien, a renowned winemaker of great style, was still alive at the time, producing bottles of rare finesse and class with the help of his family. The Tempier rosé remains one of my favorite summer glasses, with the single-vineyard red wines capable of greatness and longevity.

I was taken there by Richard Olney, with our mutual friend Jill Norman, in the late 1990s. Richard had been a fond friend of the Peyraud family for years. He loved and admired the Domaine's wine, but, almost more importantly still, he adored Lulu Peyraud's wonderful cooking. I would almost go as far as to say that he may have perceived Lulu's expertise as second to none. Considering Richard's own substantial talent for cookery and wine writing has no peer, in my view, this can only be seen as praise indeed.

Watching this diminutive woman go about preparing lunch was an absolute joy. Everything was clearly happening a great deal in her kitchen on those few days, yet none of it seemed much in evidence. Quite simply, delicious food appeared at table and we ate it. No ceremony; it was just lunch as normal at the Domaine, eaten out of doors under the shade of vine trellises. Tempier rosé was poured, naturally, and olives and thick slices of *saucisson sec* were passed around.

Richard was requested to open the difficult, indigenous "violet" clams, resembling small lumps of craggy rock, with a sharp, stubby oyster knife. When pried apart, they revealed orange flesh of a unique savor. These were our first course. Simply roasted chicken, accompanied by yellow and waxy potatoes cooked in the belly of a bulbous, terracotta pot with copious amounts of deep green Provençal olive oil, followed. Whole cloves of garlic, which had softened to an unctuous fondancy, pungently seasoned the dish. "Best potatoes I can remember," I think I said at the time.

But it was to be the braised fennel served at the second lunch—with a couple of enormous baked bream—that really blew my socks off. Again, it was olive oil and garlic that, respectively, were the chosen emollient and aromatic nuance. A splash of white wine provided lubrication. During the fennel's slow braising, the wine gently emulsified with the oil, producing a lotion of perfection. And, as I reflected at the time, these were treats eaten every single day, in that perfect place.

When I asked Lulu quite how she had put the fennel together, she typically delivered something along the lines of this:

"Well, you know, just quarter the fennel, color it a little in plenty of olive oil, put in some sliced garlic, add wine while the pot is hot, season, put on the lid, and cook it in the oven until soft and very tender." Would that all recipes were so eloquently put . . .

Celery hearts can be prepared in a similar way to Lulu Peyraud's dish above, or you could follow the recipe on page 78, which utilizes an intensely flavored porcini juice. In all cases with celery—and whether eaten raw or cooked—I would always advise peeling the outer stalks of hearts, and, when using the larger outside stalks, peel all of them.

Cream of fennel soup with garlic butter

serves 4

◈ Note that the recipe for the garlic butter will give you much more than you need for the soup. Apart from the impracticality of making a small amount, garlic butter keeps in the freezer very well and is useful to have around—delicious, instant garlic bread or with mushrooms, for instance.

2 tablespoons olive oil

2 small onions, peeled and chopped

1 fennel bulb approx.
¾ pound, trimmed and chopped

1 teaspoon fennel seeds

1 medium potato, peeled and chopped

3 cups stock

salt and freshly ground white pepper

⅔ cup whipping cream

for the garlic butter

1 cup (2 sticks) softened butter

5 cloves garlic, peeled and minced

1 cup parsley leaves, minced

2 teaspoons Pernod

¾ teaspoon salt

¼ teaspoon black pepper

good pinch of cayenne pepper

3 or 4 drops Tabasco

Heat the olive oil in a roomy pan, add the onions, and gently cook for 20 minutes or so until soft, but not colored. Add the chopped fennel with the seeds, cover, and allow to gently stew for 10 minutes. Add the potato and pour in the stock. Season and bring to a simmer. Cover and cook for 30 minutes, or until the vegetables are almost falling apart.

Meanwhile, to make the garlic butter, simply mix everything together in a bowl, place on a sheet of waxed paper, and roll up into a cylinder. Wrap in foil to secure the package and put into the freezer to firm up.

Purée the soup well in a blender, then push through a fine strainer into a clean pan. Add the cream and gently reheat. Pour into hot soup bowls and pop a slice of garlic butter onto the surface of each, to melt in.

Fennel salad with lemon & olive oil

serves 4

❖ A restaurant kitchen has the distinct advantage of a heavy-duty deli slicer for cutting fennel into the wispiest of wafer-thin shavings. In a domestic kitchen, one of those razor-sharp Japanese mandolin hand-slicers is the best option. Cut the fennel into quarters before slicing, to fit the width of the blade.

4 small, very fresh bulbs of fennel, trimmed, reserving a few fronds if attached

Maldon sea salt and freshly ground pepper

juice of 1 lemon

2 teaspoons Pernod

4 tablespoons extra-virgin olive oil

Thinly slice the fennel and lay out in a large shallow dish so that it is almost in a single layer. Season and sprinkle the lemon juice and Pernod over. Leave to macerate in a cool place for about 1 hour.

Stir together briefly and once more lay out the slices of fennel; they will now have softened up somewhat. Spoon the olive oil evenly over the fennel. Chop up any reserved feathery fronds and sprinkle over the surface to serve.

Braised fennel & celeriac with pastis

serves 4

❖ I know that the interloper celeriac (or celery root), is not strictly "celery." However, they are of the same family; and, braised together with fennel, it produces a dish of rare subtlety with deliciously molten textures.

2 fennel bulbs, trimmed

1 medium celeriac (celery root)

2 to 3 tablespoons olive oil

salt and freshly ground pepper

3 tablespoons butter

2 to 3 tablespoons pastis (preferably Ricard)

⅓ cup white wine

juice of 1 small lemon

2 tablespoons chopped parsley

Preheat the oven to 300°F. Cut the fennel lengthwise into 8 wedges. Peel the celeriac and cut into fat "French-fry" shapes. Heat the olive oil in a lidded, ovenproof cooking pot. Add the fennel and celeriac, season, and gently turn them in the oil until lightly gilded, about 15 minutes or so.

Add the butter and allow to froth, then turn down the heat. Season and add the pastis and wine. Spoon these juices over the vegetables, add the lemon juice, and allow to bubble gently. Now cover and bake in the oven for about 1 hour, until really soft and meltingly tender. Stir in the chopped parsley and serve directly from the pot.

Celery hearts in mushroom juice, vermouth & tarragon

serves 4

✤ One of my late father's Christmas contributions was to always braise some celery to accompany the turkey. I never knew exactly what he did to it, but this is my version, in memoriam.

²/₃ cup dried porcini mushrooms

1 cup hot stock

3 tablespoons butter

4 celery hearts, outer stalks peeled

1 tablespoon tarragon vinegar

1 small garlic clove, bruised

¼ cup vermouth (fragrant Noilly Prat is ideal)

1 tablespoon chopped tarragon, plus a little extra for garnish

pinch of celery salt

freshly ground white pepper

Preheat the oven to 350°F. Put the dried porcini in a bowl, pour on the stock, and leave to soak for 15 minutes. Melt the butter in an ovenproof cast-iron dish. Add the celery and gently stew until lightly colored, then add the vinegar. Allow to bubble and reduce to almost nothing, then add the porcini and stock. Bring to a boil and slip in the garlic, together with the vermouth, tarragon, celery salt, and pepper.

Cover with foil and braise in the oven for 40 minutes to 1 hour, turning the celery over halfway through. Check from time to time that there is enough liquid, lowering the temperature and adding a little more stock if things start to look too dry.

To serve, lift out the deliciously limp celery, place it on a hot serving dish, strain the juices over, and sprinkle with extra tarragon. Surprisingly good draped over a serving of nicely old-fashioned creamed potatoes.

Curry "essence"

✤ This curry essence from Constance Spry's Coronation chicken recipe is the one I have always used. For me, it is correct and authentic. You won't need all of it for the salad, but it will keep in a screw-top jar in the refrigerator for 3 to 4 weeks. It is also used in Oeufs mollets à l'indienne (see page 191).

1 tablespoon sunflower oil

½ cup chopped onion

2 teaspoons good-quality Madras curry powder

1 heaping teaspoon tomato paste

²/₃ cup red wine

½ cup water

1 bay leaf

salt, sugar, a little pepper

juice of ½ lemon

2 tablespoons apricot jam or mango chutney

Heat the oil in a pan and gently stew the onion until transparent. Add the curry powder and cook for a few minutes longer. Stir in the tomato paste and cook for a few moments, then add all the other ingredients. Bring to a simmer and cook for another 10 to 15 minutes. Strain through a fine strainer, pressing it through with a small ladle. Allow to cool.

Crisp celery & apple salad in curry cream dressing

serves 2

❀ To fashion the curry cream sauce for this, you will first need to make the curry "essence" (left), as I like to refer to it.

2 Granny Smith apples, peeled

4 crisp celery stalks, peeled

1 tablespoon golden raisins, plumped for 10 minutes in a little boiling water

generous squeeze of lemon juice

²⁄₃ cup heavy cream

2 to 3 tablespoons curry essence, or to taste (see left)

cayenne pepper

Cut the apples and celery into thick matchsticks. Carefully mix together with the raisins and lemon juice in a roomy bowl. Chill thoroughly for 30 minutes.

In another smaller bowl, beat together the cream and curry essence until loosely thickened. Fold into the apple and celery, turn into a serving dish, and sprinkle lightly with cayenne.

A perfect light lunch eaten out of doors—and relatively healthful. So promptly ruin that with a nice cold beer or two.

Lettuce & Cucumber

My friend Rowley Leigh, chef and coproprietor of Le Café Anglais, in London's Bayswater, serves a perfect green salad. He calls it "lettuce heart salad" and that is exactly what it is: carefully rinsed and dried, pale yellow leaves taken from a round lettuce (like a Boston lettuce), slightly separated and then each one dressed with just the correct amount of a judicious vinaigrette—and nothing else *at all*!

Some might say that if a salad is green, it may include such items as sliced cucumber and green pepper, or watercress and arugula. Well, I absolutely loathe any such thing, but the maker would be right; the items listed are all green, after all. However, a green salad, for me, will always be that which Rowley does so beautifully. So much, in fact, do I enjoy this salad, that it makes a perfect first course all on its own, even though there is a huge offering of other delicacies upon which to feast.

The round lettuce is a delicious, simply flavored variety and one that will be almost unknown, these days, to the munchers of pre-packed mixed leaves, so easy to just tip into a bowl and give a splash of dressing from a bottle. Okay, I am no snob, but in late spring and the summer months, when the homegrown round lettuce comes into its own, there seems little excuse not to quickly wash and spin the hearts of this fresh little lettuce, rather than to rely upon the easy route of the ubiquitous bag.

And to talk further of simple salads, the cucumber comes into its own when treated in this way. As far as I know, they still serve an impeccable *salade de concombres* at the legendary, old Parisian bistrot Allard—a bistro deluxe, which boasted two Michelin stars when Madame Allard was at the stove long ago. The cucumber is peeled, cut in half lengthwise, its seeds are removed, then it is thinly sliced into half-moons. It is then salted and left to disgorge its juices for a couple of hours or so. Once squeezed dry in a dish towel, it is dressed with a light mustard vinaigrette made with salad oil, *not* olive oil, and served sprinkled with a little finely chopped chervil or parsley. Here, once again, the salad is offered on the menu only during the summer.

Some say that Caesar Cardini, the creator of Caesar Salad, did not, in fact, include anchovies in his impromptu original. Well, be that as it may . . . Naturally, there are none in the following recipe either. And furthermore, depending on how strict a vegetarian one is, the use of Worcestershire sauce should also be avoided, including, as it surely does, anchovies in its maceration process.

However, you will be thrilled to know that for those wishing to be absolutely strict, I have devised a nifty alternative to Worcestershire sauce using mushroom ketchup (or sauce), which is available from The British Shoppe [www.britishfoodandteas.com]: simply mix 1 teaspoon Tabasco and 1 heaping teaspoon superfine sugar into 1/3 cup of mushroom ketchup and shake to dissolve the sugar. If wishing to compare, you will be pleasantly surprised by the similarity. Double or triple the quantities and make up a larger batch for frequent use, if you like. Naturally, it keeps for ages.

Caesar salad

serves 4

◈ A sourdough baguette is very good for making the croutons here. *Please* resist the urge to "shave" the Parmesan, which misses the point of the dish, as the cheese really needs to become an integral part of the dressing.

2 tablespoons butter

2 tablespoons olive oil

2 garlic cloves, peeled and crushed

3 slices good bread, cubed

salt and freshly ground pepper

2 large eggs

3 or 4 crisp hearts of romaine

⅓ cup freshly grated Parmesan

for the dressing

3 garlic cloves, peeled and crushed with ½ teaspoon salt, to a paste

2 teaspoons lemon juice

2 to 3 teaspoons Worcestershire sauce, or my alternative (see page 81)

freshly ground pepper

½ cup extra–virgin olive oil

Preheat the oven to 350°F. In a small pan, warm the butter and olive oil gently with the garlic and allow to infuse for 5 minutes or so. Strain the oily butter into a bowl. Add the bread, season, and toss with your hands, then lift out onto paper towels. Scatter the bread cubes on a baking tray and bake for about 10 minutes until crisp and golden.

Add the eggs to a pan of boiling water and boil for 2 minutes, then immediately drain and cool them under cold running water. Now crack each one open and scoop out the runny egg into a bowl. Break up with a fork until it is sloppy.

To make the dressing, in the bowl in which you will serve the salad, mix the garlic with the lemon juice, Worcestershire sauce, and plenty of pepper. Whisk in the extra-virgin olive oil until emulsified.

Separate the lettuce leaves and wash in very cold water, then spin or shake dry. Now briefly toss the croutons in the dressing so they absorb a little of it, and then add the lettuce and sloppy eggs. Lightly toss together and sprinkle with Parmesan to serve.

Boston lettuce salad with tarragon cream dressing

serves 6

❖ The tarragon cream dressing originates from one of my old Cordon Bleu magazines, where it is used to dress pears, as a sweet-savory first course. An unusual pairing (sorry), one might think, but strangely delicious.

4 or 5 heads Boston lettuce, trimmed of all floppy outer greenery

½ cucumber, peeled and sliced

6 scallions, trimmed and sliced into short lengths

6 radishes, trimmed, washed, and quartered

4 boiled eggs, peeled and quartered or sliced

1 or 2 bunches of watercress, depending on size, washed and dried

for the dressing

2 large eggs

2 teaspoons superfine sugar

3 tablespoons tarragon vinegar

pinch of salt

1 cup whipping cream

1 tablespoon chopped tarragon

a little milk (optional)

First make the dressing. Put the eggs, sugar, vinegar, and salt in the top of a double boiler, or in a glass bowl suspended over a pan of barely simmering water, and beat together, using an electric hand whisk for the speediest result. Continue until the mixture is thick and mousselike; the beaters should leave a thick trail when the whisk is lifted. Remove from the heat and continue beating until lukewarm. Cool.

Loosely whip the cream and fold into the dressing, together with the chopped tarragon; if you feel the dressing is a touch too thick, thin with a little milk.

For the salad, separate the lettuce leaves and carefully wash in very cold water, then spin or shake dry and lay out onto a handsome, large platter. Attractively arrange the cucumber, scallions, radishes, and eggs over the leaves. Pick the watercress into small sprigs and strew over the salad. Spoon the dressing over and serve at once.

Cucumber, melon & tomato salad

serves 4

❖ Having learned to cook through the 1970s, I have a soft spot for the funny old melon baller. If you don't have one, or have no intention of owning such a thing, then cut the melon into eight boat shapes, remove the flesh with a sharp knife, and cut into small wedges.

½ pound small, ripe tomatoes, cored

1 cucumber, about 10 inches long, peeled

1 melon, about 1 pound, cut in half and seeded

salt and freshly ground pepper

4 teaspoons raspberry vinegar

⅓ cup (scant) extra-virgin olive oil

2 teaspoons chopped chives

1 tablespoon shredded mint

Put the tomatoes into a bowl, pour on boiling water, and count to ten, then drain. Peel the tomatoes, cut them in half, and place in a bowl.

Cut the cucumber in half and then slice each piece lengthwise in two. Scoop the seeds out, using a teaspoon (or melon baller), then slice the 4 lengths into somewhat thick slices with a slight diagonal bias, simply for a more pleasing look. Add to the tomatoes.

Make balls or wedges from the melon and add to the tomatoes and cucumber. Season lightly and add the remaining ingredients. Toss gently and leave in the refrigerator to macerate for at least 30 minutes before serving.

Eat with toasted slices of baguette, delicately rubbed with a cut garlic clove and brushed with olive oil.

Buttered cucumber with cress & mint

serves 2

❖ This simple, summery and fragrant little dish is very pleasing eaten warm with slices of thinly buttered rye bread, spread with cream cheese.

1 cucumber, peeled

2 tablespoons butter, plus a little extra to finish

salt and freshly ground pepper

small pinch of sugar

1½ cups mustard cress or chopped watercress

1 tablespoon chopped mint

1 to 2 teaspoons white wine vinegar

Cut the cucumber in half and then slice each piece lengthwise in two. Cut the 4 lengths into thickish slices, with a slight diagonal bias. Melt the butter in a deep skillet and add the cucumber. Season, add the sugar, and allow to gently stew for a few minutes until softened but not soggy.

Sprinkle the mustard cress or chopped watercress and the mint all over the surface. Turn up the heat, toss the cucumber around with a wooden spoon, and mix well. Finally, add the vinegar and a touch more butter, just to add a final gloss. Turn into a shallow dish and serve warm.

Garlic & Shallots

As it seeps out of early morning metropolitan restaurant kitchen vents when office-bound folk are on their way to their desks in giant, equality open-plan rooms stacked one on top of the other, the aroma of chopped garlic and shallots stewing together in butter defies eloquent description. As they pass by the busy *commis* chef's first shift in his hot basement, these striding, be-suited types, might mutter thus: "*Mmmm . . .*" or "*Ahhhh . . . that smells soooo good!*"

These two intimate alliums begin so many savory stews and braises that it is difficult to imagine such dishes without this familiar overture. Moreover, not to marry them seems inconceivable to the home cook who enjoys being in his/her kitchen, making family meals with pleasure, day in, day out. Admittedly a rare thing, these days, but such folk do still exist.

Indian vegetarian cookery, to generalize, is a case in point—for the onion/garlic pairing, as well as the regular making of family meals. Ghee, rather than butter, would be the grease of choice here, so that a higher temperature may be achieved, as cooks of that country prefer to take the cooking of both onion and garlic to extremes. And I have always believed that this is where we amateurs of curry making—to use a prosaic description—fall short: we simply dare not deeply burnish, and therefore our attempts often fall short of authenticity.

I recall a stew of eggplant that I once ate in a simple Formica-topped table establishment in Southall, in the far west of London (almost adjacent to Heathrow Airport's runway), together with an Australian friend who adored Indian food but who was bereft of such delights in Sydney. It was an exact example of the benefit given to the bland eggplant by deep golden shreds of onions and garlic.

The slippery-sloppy fingers of that naturally spongy vegetable had, you see, soaked up all those toasted flavors, so taking it onto quite another plane. Yes, there was also finely minced fresh ginger and cumin seed in there, too, as well as lots of chopped cilantro leaf and green chili, but the basis of this wonderfully oily dish relied, most heavily, upon that richly golden onion and garlic.

There is much discussion as to whether the wispy, often acrid green germ within a garlic clove should be removed prior to cooking; I am quite convinced that the Asian restaurant cook would not bother to do so. A great deal of garlic, after all, is prepared daily in all such kitchens; and, what with the chore of peeling hundreds of cloves as it is, the very idea of splitting each one in half and teasing out said green germ would be anathema to the poor kitchen lad.

Personally, I would recommend removing the germ if preparing more subtle European dishes, particularly if using garlic raw, and especially if the garlic seems a little less than sprightly; if the cloves are at all dry and leathery, they should be discarded anyway, and fresher garlic sourced at once.

However, I have discovered it is often best to find big fat heads of fresh, new crop garlic in the spring, purchase plenty, store them carefully, and keep a check on how they are faring over time. I have been pleasantly surprised to discover that the germ is rarely, if ever, revealed by the time of exhaustion.

New-crop garlic, saffron & tomato quiche

serves 4

◈ It should be noted that the quiche filling will be far too strong if it is made with anything other than fresh, new-crop garlic cloves, however many times they have been blanched in boiling water.

for the pie crust

¾ cup (scant) all-purpose flour

4½ tablespoons (generous ½ stick) butter, cut into cubes

pinch of salt

1 to 2 tablespoons ice water

for the filling

20 peeled new-crop garlic cloves

salt and freshly ground pepper

7 ounces ripe tomatoes, peeled and chopped

⅓ cup milk

1 teaspoon saffron threads

2 large eggs

1 large egg yolk

⅓ cup sour cream

⅓ cup heavy cream

⅜ cup (rounded) light cream cheese

¼ cup freshly grated Parmesan

For the pie crust, put the flour, butter, and salt into a food processor and briefly blend together until the mixture resembles fine bread crumbs. Now tip into a large, roomy bowl and gently mix in the water, using cool hands or a knife, until well amalgamated. Knead together, then put into a plastic bag and rest in the refrigerator for at least 1 hour before rolling.

For the filling, put the garlic cloves into a small pan, cover with water, and bring to a boil. Drain and refresh with cold water, then repeat. Drain and refresh again, cover with water once more, add a little salt, and simmer for several minutes until very soft. Drain and set aside.

Put the tomatoes and a little seasoning into a stainless steel pan and allow to simmer for a good half an hour or so, at least until the mixture is well reduced and jammy (it needs to be spread onto the pie crust base).

Preheat the oven to 350°F and put a baking sheet inside to heat up. Roll out the dough on a lightly floured counter, as thinly as you dare, then use to line an 8-inch, 3-inch-deep tart pan and prick the base. Line the pie crust with foil and dried beans, slide onto the hot baking sheet, and bake "blind" for about 15 minutes. Remove the foil and beans and return the pie crust to the oven for another 10 to 15 minutes until it is golden, crisp, and well cooked through, particularly the base.

Put the milk into a small pan with the saffron, warm through, and leave to infuse for 5 minutes. Blitz the eggs, egg yolk, and cooked garlic together in a food processor until smooth. Add the sour and heavy creams, the cream cheese, and Parmesan and briefly blend again. Pour into a bowl and stir in the saffron-infused milk. Season lightly.

To assemble the tart, spread the tomatoes over the pie crust and then pour in the saffron custard; you may find it less nerve-racking to half-fill the pie shell first and spoon or ladle in the rest once it is in the oven. Bake for 30 to 40 minutes, until set and pale golden on the surface. Allow to cool for at least 10 minutes before eating, as hot quiche tastes of very little.

Fresh garlic purée

makes about 1½ to 1¾ cups

❖ This purée is very good with broiled eggplants and zucchini, or with halved fennel bulbs that have been parboiled and then oven roasted. It is also delicious spread onto bruschetta and topped with sliced tomatoes or hard-boiled eggs, or both.

3 large heads of new-crop garlic

salt and freshly ground white pepper

1 cup crème fraîche or sour cream

Separate and peel the garlic cloves, then simmer in salted water until just tender; drain. Purée the garlic in a food processor, but leave a little grainy. Tip into a bowl and allow to cool completely. Add the crème fraîche and beat with a whisk until thick. Add more salt to taste and grind in plenty of white pepper.

Crisp fried shallots

❖ These shards of deeply savory onion-y-ness are wonderful when tossed into all kinds of salads. They are also good sprinkled over Welsh rarebit, or a cream of onion or leek and potato soup, in place of the more traditional croutons. Slices of garlic can be given a similar treatment, but these should not be taken as far as the shallots—more of a pale golden—as they can become horribly burned and bitter.

6 to 8 shallots, or more

oil for frying (a neutral-flavored oil, such as sunflower or peanut)

Maldon sea salt

Peel and thickly slice the shallots—to about ¼ inch thick. Put them into a deep skillet, just cover with oil, and place over medium heat. When the shallots begin to sizzle, start to stir them around with a kitchen fork, gently separating them as they cook. Keeping the heat moderate, continue to fry until they have turned a rich golden brown and are deeply shriveled up; lift one or two out and check for crispness, although they will crisp up even more, once drained. Lift out the shallots using a slotted spoon, drain on a double layer of paper towels, and sprinkle with fine sea salt.

Sweet & sour shallots

serves 4 to 6

These would be good eaten with a piping hot cauliflower and cheese (see page 34) or macaroni and cheese with tomatoes (see page 162). Since the amount of shallots here is quite a handful—well, much more than that—it is worth pouring some boiling water over them before peeling, as this eases the task. Leave in the water for a couple of minutes, then drain.

1 pound small shallots, peeled

½ cup (scant) sherry vinegar

¾ cup water

⅓ cup olive oil

1½ tablespoons tomato paste

3 tablespoons sugar

salt and freshly ground pepper

2 bay leaves

2 rosemary sprigs

⅓ cup currants

chopped parsley to garnish

Preheat the oven to 300°F. Put the shallots into a lidded, solid cooking pot. Whisk together the vinegar, water, olive oil, tomato paste, and sugar, then add salt and pepper to taste. Pour over the shallots and add the bay leaves and rosemary. Now stir in the currants, while also making sure that the shallots are submerged in the liquid.

Bring to a simmer on top of the stove and gently cook for a few minutes, stirring a little to mingle the ingredients together. Once gently bubbling, put on the lid and slide into the oven. Cook for about 1 hour 20 minutes, until the shallots are soft, but not falling apart. I suggest that you check after 1 hour, just to be sure. Serve at room temperature, sprinkled with chopped parsley.

Ginger & Scallions

It is the Chinese we must thank for the burst of flavor given by the pairing of shredded ginger and scallions. When added to various dishes from that country, they work in a similar way to golden fried onions and garlic, which combine to enhance stews, braises, and, particularly, curries. With ginger and scallions, it is most often in their raw state, or added during the last moments of cooking, where these aromatic flavors so successfully dance upon the taste buds.

Such a garnish, with a large steamed sea bass, was my first experience of fine Pekingese cooking—or Bejingese, perhaps, now—soon after I had arrived in London about thirty years ago. And it was on Willesden High Road, of all places. Here is that restaurant's Wikipedia entry:

"The Kuo Yuan was established in 1963 when a group of Chinese restaurateurs managed to convince the Chinese ambassador's chef, a Mr. Kuo from Beijing, to defect. A visit by Princess Margaret and Lord Snowdon, the Posh and Becks of their day, put both the restaurant and Chinese food on the map. It was also recommended by Egon Ronay."

And, as it so happened, it was to be on a visit with Egon Ronay himself (for whom I was working as an inspector at the time) and his friend the late, legendary Ken Lo, who later went on to open his own restaurants and who had already written several excellent books on Chinese cookery.

It was a marvelous evening, with many dishes ordered, including some that would not normally have been offered to *gweilos* (the Chinese slang for Caucasians). But it was the sea bass I particularly remember, so perfectly cooked as it was, with its pearly white flesh all moist and juicy, together with an oily dressing of soy and this great pile of just-wilting shredded ginger and scallions covering the entire fish. It was to be an important initiation to a huge learning curve, that evening, the least of it learning how to pry morsels of fish from the bone with chopsticks.

A pleasing condiment to have around is a ginger-infused vinegar. It is particularly good sprinkled onto a bowl of congee (see page 184), or any other Chinese-inspired dish, simple stir-fried noodles, or plain boiled rice, even. You can use white wine vinegar if you like, but I think it is worthwhile searching out rice wine vinegar. For ease of sprinkling, either use an old soy sauce bottle (the kind with a spout on either side of the cap).

One-third fill the chosen receptacle with very finely chopped peeled fresh ginger (a funnel is the easiest way to do this, forcing it through with a chopstick or similar), then fill up with vinegar. Leave to infuse for a week or so, shaking it about a bit from time to time, then use the infused vinegar as desired. I think it is delicious sprinkled over scrambled eggs cooked with scallions, for example, which, after all, is quite apt here.

Asian scallion, radish & cucumber salad with cashews & vermicelli

serves 4

❋ Before you start, you will need on hand both ginger syrup and sesame paste. Also, feel free to add more of one ingredient or another, and to adjust the sweet-sharp balance of the dressing.

¼ pound dried thread vermicelli (or glass noodles)

2 heaping tablespoons unsalted cashew nuts

salt

a little sunflower oil

6 radishes, trimmed

6 scallions, trimmed

1 cucumber, 7 inches long

generous handful each of cilantro and mint leaves

1 or 2 large red chilis, sliced

for the dressing

1 tablespoon ginger syrup (see below)

1 tablespoon sesame paste (see page 173)

juice of 2 limes

1 tablespoon Asian fish sauce or light soy sauce

1 tablespoon sesame oil

to garnish

2 teaspoons toasted sesame seeds

Snap the vermicelli into shorter lengths, one-third of the original, folded skein. Soak in cold water for about 30 minutes, or until well softened. Drain and return to the bowl. Now cover with boiling water, and fork and lift the noodles around for a few minutes until they have become silky, soft, and tender (eat one). Drain, rinse in cold water, and set aside.

In a small skillet, gently toast the cashews with a little salt in a little oil until golden all over. Cool, and then crush each cashew lightly with the back of a knife. Reserve.

Cut the radishes into quarters or rounds, the scallions into diagonal shreds, and the cucumber into thick matchsticks. Tip the prepared vegetables into a large bowl and add the vermicelli. Tear the cilantro and mint leaves into smaller pieces and add to the salad with the chili. Mix together with your hands to distribute everything evenly.

Now whisk the dressing ingredients together in a small bowl. Add to the salad and mix together once more with two forks, lifting and dropping the salad so that all is evenly dressed. Pile onto a shallow serving dish and sprinkle the crushed cashews and sesame seeds over. Best eaten pleasantly chilled, with warm sake or ice-cold beer.

Ginger syrup

2 cups (scant) granulated sugar

1½ cups water

finely pared zest of 1 lemon (use a potato peeler)

1½ cups peeled and coarsely grated fresh ginger

Dissolve the sugar in the water in a pan over medium heat, then bring to a boil and cook for 2 minutes. Immediately add the lemon zest and ginger and stir together. Bring back to aboil for a few seconds and then pour into a bowl. Cover and leave to infuse overnight.

The following day, add 2 tablespoons water and warm through until liquid and pourable. Strain through a sieve and press on the solids with the back of a ladle to extract all the ginger and lemon flavors. Pour the syrup into a screw-top jar and store in the refrigerator until needed, where it will keep for several weeks.

A kind of hot & sour soup with bean curd

serves 4

◈ This serves as an almost instant, meat-free version of the famously perky Chinese soup. However, look upon it as a soup in its own right—albeit with a nod or two to the original. It is important to use white pepper here, for its unique flavor and heat.

⅔ cup dried shitake mushrooms

1 cup hot water

1¼ cups very thinly sliced leek, mostly the white part

3 cups stock

1½ to 2 tablespoons black Chinese vinegar, rice vinegar, or sherry vinegar, to taste

½ cup (scant) light soy sauce

⅓ cup Chinese rice wine

1 tablespoon fresh ginger julienne strips (fine matchsticks)

½ tablespoon minced garlic

1 cup frozen corn kernels

1 cup frozen peas

2 teaspoons freshly ground white pepper

5 ounces fresh bean curd, cut into small cubes

2 teaspoons arrowroot, slaked with 1 tablespoon cold water

to garnish

sliced scallions

sesame oil

cilantro leaves, roughly chopped

First soak the shitake mushrooms in the hot water for 30 minutes, then drain, reserving the liquid for the soup, and slice the shitake. Strain the mushroom liquid through a cheesecloth-lined strainer to remove any grit.

Simmer the leek in the stock and mushroom liquid in a large pan until soft. Add the rest of the ingredients, except the bean curd and arrowroot. Bring up to a boil and then simmer for 15 minutes.

Stir in the bean curd, followed by the arrowroot, and continue cooking for a few more minutes until the soup is lightly thickened and shiny; don't cook for too long, as arrowroot has a tendency to break down and the soup will thin out.

Decant into hot soup bowls and add a touch of sliced scallion, sesame oil, and chopped cilantro to each serving.

A ginger & scallion dressing for broiled eggplants

serves 4

❧ The best eggplants for utilizing this sweet and sour dressing most successfully are the elongated, pale purple, and thin-skinned variety. I have tried the recipe with the common or garden black-skinned ones, but with disappointment.

1 cup Chinese rice wine

¼ cup (scant) light soy sauce

1 tablespoon ginger syrup (see page 94)

piece of fresh ginger, approx. 1 inch in diameter and 2 inches long, peeled and chopped

1 tablespoon chopped scallions

2 garlic cloves, peeled and chopped

1 tablespoon rice wine vinegar

2 teaspoons sesame seeds

to serve

4 large eggplants

oil for shallow- or deep-frying

chopped cilantro leaves to garnish (optional)

Pour the rice wine into a saucepan, bring up to a boil, and ignite. Turn down to a more relaxed simmer and, once the flames have died down, continue to reduce the liquid until about half its original volume. Allow to cool completely, then pour into a small food processor. Add the remaining ingredients and purée until fairly smooth. Pour into a small bowl.

To prepare the eggplants, cut them in half lengthwise. Heat the oil in a suitable pan and fry the eggplants for about 10 to 15 minutes (less if deep-frying), turning as necessary, until nearly tender. Place, cut side down, on paper towels to drain well.

Now preheat the broiler to medium and lay the eggplant halves in a heatproof dish, cut side uppermost. Slash the surface in a few places with a sharp knife and then spoon some of the dressing over, pushing it down into the eggplant flesh. Broil for a few moments, then add a little more dressing. Continue to broil the eggplants until golden and drenched in dressing; a modicum of residue will also have collected in the dish, which you may allow to become deliciously sticky and aromatic.

Serve two eggplant halves per person and, if desired, garnish with chopped cilantro leaves.

Chilis & Avocados

It was on a trip to New York last year that I first met Mario Batali. He had very kindly hosted a splendid dinner at his restaurant Babbo, together with a mutual friend of ours and other jolly guests, too. So, it was a happy party and, as the evening wore on, became positively vivacious. Mario had also laid on some wonderful old Italian wines, which included, as far as I remember— and which is difficult—a 1958 Barolo. But the food was splendid and memorable.

One particular dish drew my attention: a braise of squid, or calamari, cooked "in the style of a Sicilian lifeguard." "Could I just have the lifeguard and hold the squid, please?" I quipped. Anyway, Mario said that the squid had been on the menu since Babbo's opening night, eleven years ago, but that he now stirred in a jalapeño chili relish just before serving the dish. Well, let me tell you, it was just marvelous! The relish recipe follows, and also appears in other chapters. Mario says he loves it so much that he often spreads it thickly on toast.

Learning of this delicious paste further urged me to discover more about jalapeños. I have found their taste to be unlike other green chili peppers, in that although it is fiery, the flavor emerges as rich and fruity, together with a juiciness that is so often missing in other varieties.

My first look at an avocado was on Christmas morning when I was about six years old. Mum had bought Dad a food hamper from the very grand Kendals department store food hall, in Manchester, for one of his Christmas presents. Kendals, then (1960), was possibly the only grocers in the entire northwest of England where an avocado could be purchased. We were all very excited for Dad since, at the time, his cooking skills were becoming more and more exotic. Paella, moules marinières, Indian curries, and sweet 'n' sour pork were making regular appearances on family Saturday nights, or whenever Mum was in dinner party mode. It is little wonder some of this would eventually rub off onto someone else . . .

Mario Batali's almond & jalapeño relish

makes about 1¼ cups

⅓ cup whole almonds

5 ounces green jalapeño peppers

1 small red onion, peeled

1 teaspoon Maldon sea salt

⅓ cup extra-virgin olive oil

pinch of sugar

Roughly chop the almonds, peppers, and onion and put into a small food processor with the rest of the ingredients. Grind everything together until smooth-ish, but don't take it to an absolute purée. This relish is best eaten or used fresh, the day it is made, but it can be frozen in small containers.

Chilled avocado soup with tomatillo salsa

serves 4

❖ One of the most delicious and delicate cold soups I know—and so very easy to make. The salsa may also be made with tomatoes.

for the salsa

5 ounces tomatillos (or tomatoes)

1 jalapeño pepper, seeded (for less heat) or not

½ red onion, peeled

small handful of cilantro leaves, chopped

juice of 1 lime, or more

salt

pinch of sugar

for the soup

2 or 3 ripe, chilled Hass avocados

⅔ cup chilled stock, or more to taste

1½ cups chilled buttermilk

few shakes of green Tabasco

juice of 1 small lime, or more

salt

pinch of cayenne pepper

to finish (optional)

a little sour cream, thinned with a little milk

To make the salsa, mince the tomatillos (or tomatoes), chili, and onion and put into a bowl. Add the rest of the ingredients and mix everything together. Check the seasoning, adding another squeeze of lime juice if you wish. Leave to macerate while you make the soup.

For the soup, halve the avocados, remove the peel and pit, then coarsely chop the flesh. Place in a blender (preferable to a food processor here) with all the other ingredients and whiz until very smooth indeed. Even so, I always pass the soup through a fine strainer just to make sure, but then "pedantic" is my middle name. Put to chill in the refrigerator for at least 30 minutes, or longer.

If, once chilled, the soup is too thick for your liking, thin with a touch more chilled stock. Taste for seasoning and add a little more lime juice if you think it is needed.

Pour into chilled soup bowls and spoon a small pile of salsa into the center of each serving. If you like, drizzle with some thinned sour cream, too.

Guacamole

serves 2 to 4, as a snack

◈ I love this particular method for making guacamole, as it turns out so very green. The inclusion of fresh green tomatillos helps, but you could use tomatoes instead and forgo the singular, verdant hue.

1 medium onion, peeled and chopped

juice of 1 small lime, or more

salt

1 or 2 jalapeño peppers, seeded (for less heat) or not, chopped

generous handful of cilantro leaves

1 or 2 tomatillos depending on size (or tomatoes)

2 or 3 ripe Hass avocados, about 1 pound or more

Put the onion, lime juice, salt, chilis, and cilantro into a small food processor and purée until smooth-ish. Tip into a fine strainer suspended over a bowl and force out all the juice from the pulp using the back of a ladle.

Slice the tomatillos and then mince them. Halve the avocados, remove the peel and pit, then coarsely chop the flesh. Add the avocados and tomatillos to the onion chili juice, toss to mix, and check for salt.

Chill the guacamole until ready to serve. Eat with tortilla chips, naturally, and maybe a margarita, or two . . .

Red pepper & potato stew with jalapeño relish

serves 2, generously

◈ The jalapeño relish transforms this simple vegetable stew.

¾ pound medium–small waxy potatoes, peeled

¾ pound red bell peppers

2 tablespoons olive oil

1 medium onion, peeled and sliced

3 garlic cloves, peeled and sliced

1 bay leaf

3 strips of lemon zest

salt

1 cup stock

2 teaspoons almond & jalapeño relish (see page 99), or to taste

a little chopped cilantro (optional)

Preheat the oven to 350°F. Cut the potatoes lengthwise into quarters. Core and seed the peppers and then cut into pieces similar in size to the potatoes.

In a roomy, lidded cooking pot, heat the olive oil and add the onion. Cook gently until softened and then tip in the potatoes, peppers, garlic, bay, lemon zest, and salt to taste. Stir together well and add the stock.

Bring the pot up to a simmer, then cover the vegetables with a piece of waxed paper, cut to fit, and put on the lid. Cook in the oven for 40 minutes, or until the potatoes are tender and the red peppers are nice and soft, too.

Stir in the jalapeño relish, being careful not to break up the potatoes, and sprinkle the chopped cilantro over, if using. Serve directly from the pot into warmed soup plates. Eat with spoons.

Chili con carnevale

serves 4

◈ I am quite pleased over the naming of this dish. *Carnevale*, from the Italian/Latin, is the original form of the word "carnival:" *carne* "meat;" *vale* "leave." In other words, "goodbye to meat" on the last day before Lent begins, which is also called Shrove Tuesday and Mardi Gras: "Fat Tuesday." *Capiche*?

The chili powder I prefer to use in the recipe is *not* "pure" chili powder, or hot cayenne pepper; rather, it is a chili powder "mix," which includes oregano and cumin as seasoning ingredients. Also, I like to add a little more cumin and oregano, too. Together with the jalapeño relish stirred in at the end, it really makes this meatless chili a memorable one.

3 tablespoons olive oil

1 large onion, peeled and chopped

2 celery stalks, peeled and chopped

1 green bell pepper, seeded and chopped

1 red bell pepper, seeded and chopped

2 large, flat mushrooms, chopped

4 garlic cloves, peeled and minced

1 tablespoon hot chili powder (see above)

1 teaspoon ground cumin

½ teaspoon dried oregano

1 tablespoon tomato paste

3 cups canned red kidney beans, drained

2 cups canned chopped tomatoes

⅔ cup stock

salt

1 to 2 tablespoons almond & jalapeño relish (see page 99)

to garnish

sour cream

tomato salsa (see page 100)

thinly sliced scallions

Preheat the oven to 310°F. Heat the olive oil in a solid cooking pot and add the onion, celery, both peppers, mushrooms, and garlic. Fry gently, stirring occasionally, for about 20 to 30 minutes, until well colored.

Stir in the chili powder, cumin, and oregano, and continue to cook gently for 5 minutes, so "cooking out" the spices. Add the tomato paste and allow that to sizzle for a few minutes, until it changes color from bright red to more of a deep rust.

Now tip in the beans, canned tomatoes, and stock. Stir together until well amalgamated and add a little salt (the chili will reduce somewhat during its cooking time, so beware). Cook, uncovered, in the oven for about 1 hour, taking the pot out a couple of times to gently stir the chili, while being careful not to break up the beans.

Remove from the oven and place over very low heat. You will now notice that the oil has settled on the surface. Well, I like to leave it there and then stir it in, but if you wish for a less oily chili, remove it with a few paper towels applied to the surface area. For me, the finished chili should be fairly thick, so if the mixture remains too sloppy, allow it to reduce until a desired consistency has been reached.

Check for salt and stir in the jalapeño relish, to taste. Serve in individual bowls and add as much or as little garnish as you like.

Eggplants & Peppers

Eggplants have always played a big part in my life. I love the look of them, all of them—so much so that an entire shelf in my living room is given over to inedible, decorative examples. After many years of generous gifts from friends, with a few found by me, this purple-black corner space is now entirely filled. The only drawback, I guess, is that they take an age to dust . . .

It has been suggested that the earliest known variety of eggplant is the small white one, hence the name "eggplant." Some perfect examples truly resemble a white egg, save the obvious stalk. Other varieties followed, or maybe they were already waiting in the wings, such as the tiny, slightly bitter green pea eggplant and a larger, also white-ish one, about the size of a squash ball, from Thailand. There is also the long, pale purple, and deliciously thin-skinned, generally Asian variety—although relatively common in my West London, Middle Eastern grocer's, too. These are absolutely the ones to use for all recipes where the skin is as important as the flesh within, in that it becomes indiscernible, once cooked (see pages 108–9.)

One of my favorites is the lilac, purple, and creamy giant ball of an eggplant, from Sicily. Although this is also a fairly thin-skinned variety, in that country (as all Sicilians would have you believe) you would almost never consume a dish of these unpeeled. I approve of this, especially when the vegetable is unadorned—say slices that have been simply broiled or cooked in olive oil, as part of an antipasti. Who needs to eat the skin? Of course, this is even more relevant when using the common, mostly hothouse Dutch-grown black beasts that are all most of us in Britain can find. They ain't bad, but they are one dimensional when compared with Sicilian monsters, with which one could almost play soccer.

Provençal, sun-drenched black-skinned eggplants and similarly ripened red bell peppers, are just two of the ingredients that go toward the fabrication of a colorful ratatouille. A peerless vegetable dish if ever there was one, which I prefer to eat cold or at least at room temperature. So, why no recipe from this cook? Well, you know, I think I would rather talk it through this time, rather than list and measure.

One of the best, if not *the* best, is a ratatouille I have eaten many times at the tiny La Merenda restaurant, in Nice, on a small street running up from the seafront and just by the market. I cannot offer a telephone number, as it does not have one, nor does it accept payment by credit card or check.

Dominique Le Stanc, chef-proprietor, makes a ratatouille that he serves only in late spring and summer, when all the components are at their very best. He uses red and yellow bell peppers, small and tender eggplants and zucchini, sweet onions, fabulously ripe tomatoes, which—sensibly—he does not skin, as to so do would allow them to melt away into the dish, as sauce. I believe that he cooks the ingredients separately, slightly burnishing them in local olive oil, then mixes them together and turns the tomatoes through the other vegetables for just a few minutes until they only just collapse. To finish the dish—and this is his masterstroke—a small spoonful of basil, garlic, and olive oil, mashed to a paste, is then poured over each plateful. Play around with that, please, won't you?

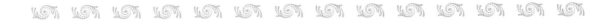

Caponata

serves 4

✧ It was going to be either this Sicilian dish, or the ratatouille, that would be given a full recipe or a talk-through. The caponata won by a short head—and it is a little more complicated and has many more ingredients, too.

2 large eggplants

salt

1 large red onion, peeled, halved, and thickly sliced

4 celery stalks, peeled, halved lengthwise, and sliced into short lengths

1 small yellow bell pepper, halved, seeded, and thickly sliced

1 small red bell pepper, halved, seeded, and thickly sliced

5 to 6 tablespoons olive oil

½ cup (scant) water

3 tablespoons red wine vinegar

1 rounded tablespoon sugar

2 teaspoons tomato paste

1 tablespoon raisins

about 12 green olives, pitted and halved

1 tablespoon capers, drained and lightly squeezed dry

1 tablespoon pine nuts

freshly ground white pepper

Peel the eggplants and thickly slice them into semicircles. Spread them out on a kitchen counter and sprinkle with enough salt to season generously. Gather them up in your hands, mingle together in a colander, place on a plate, and leave to exude their juices for at least 40 minutes.

Meanwhile, using a skillet, and in four separate stages, gently stew the onion, celery, yellow and red bell peppers separately, each in 1 tablespoon of the olive oil, until softened and only *just* colored. For the fifth stage, wash and dry the eggplants and similarly soften in olive oil. Place all five vegetables in a bowl and mingle together.

Now add the water, vinegar, sugar, tomato paste, and raisins to the skillet. Bring to a boil and simmer for several minutes until lightly thickened and the raisins have plumped somewhat. Stir in the olives and capers and tip the entire contents of the skillet into the bowl of vegetables.

Gently heat the pine nuts in a dry skillet until golden brown. Add them to the caponata, season with pepper to taste, and check for salt. Lubricate with a little more olive oil, if you think it warrants it, and serve at room temperature.

Red pepper mousse with garlic toasts

serves 4 to 5

◈ The main reason I suggest using bottled Spanish piquillo peppers in this recipe is that their flavor is more intense than those of fresh ones which have been baked and peeled by you. Okay, it also makes the job easier … But it is the taste that remains paramount, here. Before processing, be sure to remove any little black bits from the peppers if they have been broiled.

for the mousses

5 to 6 ounces ripe tomatoes, coarsely chopped

1 rounded tablespoon agar flakes (see page 9)

1 cup (rounded) drained bottled Spanish piquillo peppers

pinch of cayenne pepper

½ teaspoon celery salt

½ teaspoon sugar

1 teaspoon red wine vinegar

½ cup whipping cream

for the garlic toasts

allow 2 long slices of rustic baguette (cut on the diagonal), per person

1 garlic clove, peeled and halved

Maldon sea salt and freshly ground pepper

olive oil for brushing

Place the tomatoes in a small pan and sprinkle the agar flakes over. Warm through over low heat, swirling the tomatoes around until they begin to wilt and release some of their juices, then stir in the slowly melting agar flakes. Allow to stew gently for a further 3 to 4 minutes.

Purée the piquillo peppers, cayenne, celery salt, sugar, and vinegar in a blender until very smooth. Add the tomatoes to the blender now (scraping out every last vestige with a spatula) and blend briefly once more. Now pass this mixture through a fine strainer into a bowl, pressing down on the solids with the back of a small ladle. Refrigerate for at least 30 minutes, or until beginning to set.

Whip the cream in another bowl, only just until soft peaks form. Now transfer the whisk to the pepper mixture and give this a brief whisking to loosen it. Carefully fold the cream into the pepper purée until well combined and without any white streaks. Decant into ramekins, smooth over the surface, and stretch a piece of plastic wrap over the top of each one. Place in the refrigerator to set, for at least 2 hours, or longer.

For the garlic toasts, toast the baguette slices until nicely burnished. Rub the cut garlic clove over each one, season lightly, and brush with olive oil.

Eat the red pepper mousse with teaspoons, occasionally spreading some of it onto the garlic toasts.

Fried eggplant with skordalia

serves 2

◈ The very nicest of Greek taverna dishes, best enjoyed as part of a late lunch and with some very cold, iced ouzo.

1 large eggplant, trimmed

salt

olive oil for shallow-frying

flour for coating

for the skordalia

1 thick slice crustless, slightly stale fresh white bread, in large cubes

²/₃ cup milk

1 garlic clove, peeled and crushed to a paste with salt

1 to 2 scant tablespoons white wine vinegar

pepper

about 3 tablespoons olive oil

Slice the eggplant into rounds, about ²/₃ inch thick. Immerse in a bowl of well-salted water and leave to soak for 30 minutes, turning the slices around from time to time.

Meanwhile, make the skordalia. Soak the bread in the milk for a few minutes until spongy. Squeeze the excess milk out with your hands and put the bread into a food processor with the garlic, vinegar, and some pepper. Pulse briefly, adding the olive oil in a thin stream, until the mixture is thick and pastelike; try not to overwork it, however, as you want to retain some of the texture of the bread.

Drain the eggplant slices in a colander, then lay out on a dish towel in one layer, but don't let them dry out; they should remain a bit wet. Now heat about a ¹/₃-inch depth of olive oil in a large skillet until hot, but not smoking. Dip each slice of eggplant in flour, shake off excess, and fry about 5 to 6 slices at a time, turning once, until golden brown on each side. Drain on paper towels.

Serve the crisp-fried eggplant slices piping hot, with the skordalia.

Broiled eggplant with pesto

serves 2

❖ An old favorite, which I could not resist including here.

1 large eggplant

about ½ cup extra-virgin olive oil

salt and freshly ground pepper

3 tablespoons pine nuts

a large bunch of basil

3 garlic cloves, peeled and crushed

3 tablespoons freshly grated pecorino or Parmesan

½ lemon, to serve

Preheat the oven to 425°F. Cut the eggplant lengthwise in half, through the stalk. Using a small, sharp knife, make a crisscross pattern across the cut surfaces, to a depth of about ¾ inch. Brush with a little of the olive oil and season. Bake in the oven for 20 to 30 minutes. The flesh should be very soft.

Meanwhile, lightly toast the pine nuts in a dry skillet, then remove from the skillet and cool. Process the basil, garlic, and pine nuts, together with a little salt and pepper, to a paste in a food processor (or use a mortar and pestle for a more authentic result). Now add enough of the olive oil to produce a loose-textured purée. Finally, briefly mix in the cheese.

Spread the pesto over the scored surfaces of the eggplant and broil until golden and bubbling. Serve with a squeeze of lemon.

Potatoes Old & New

Triple-cooked French fries, albeit delicious, are nothing more than fries cooked with a great deal of care. Why does one need to be told they are triple-cooked? The same goes for "hand-cut" French fries. Why does one need this information? Maybe restaurant kitchens want us to be wildly impressed with all of this. Just get on with the cutting and cooking is what I say.

All good French fries need to be cooked twice anyway, to make them crisp: first slow-fried in oil at a low temperature for several minutes, then finished in hot oil for about two. You can leave a few hours between these stages if that suits your timing better. When I first learned how to do this as a teenage apprentice, it reminded me of my brother and I, years before, making chips (as we British call French fries) in our chip pan at home and realizing that we could have made them much nicer than we did, had we known this trick at the time. Our fries, then, emerged limp, a deep brown on the outside, and always a little bit raw in the middle. But we ate them anyway, because using the chip pan at all was fun, exciting, and just a little bit dangerous.

Conversely, in terms of crispness and texture, one would never want the initial rustle of a chip-shop chip to last. The great joy of such a morsel is its wane from the fryer—so becoming deliciously warm and only just tinged with tiny, remaining edges of crunch—helped, of course, by having been drenched in copious shakes of malt vinegar.

Bringing some excellent fish and chips home once, and not having any malt vinegar on hand, I made the heinous mistake of using tarragon vinegar instead, this being my only choice from the pantry. So horrible were they, that they ended up in the garbage after only a couple of bites. Should have known better. Silly me.

Fragrantly, spring moving into summertime arrives for me with the first scent from a pan of new potatoes simmering with mint. So good are these tiny little marbles, once buttered, that I can eat a bowl of them all on their own—vegetarian food at its very best, I claim. When something so simple as this tastes so very good, it does not need any messing around with—the purity should be championed.

Simple new potato salad

serves 4

❖ It is important here to dress the potatoes while they are still warm. Any leftover dressing will keep well in the refrigerator.

1½ pounds new potatoes, washed

salt

for the dressing

2 tablespoons smooth Dijon mustard

2 tablespoons white wine or tarragon vinegar

salt and freshly ground pepper

2 tablespoons lukewarm water

1⅓ cups sunflower oil

2 tablespoons chopped chives or scallions

1 tablespoon minced parsley

Put the potatoes to simmer (or steam) in salted water. When cooked through, drain and leave until just cool enough to handle, then peel.

To make the dressing, put the mustard, vinegar, seasoning, and water in a blender or food processor and blitz until smooth, then start adding the oil in a thin stream. When the consistency is pale and creamy, have a taste. If you think it is too thick, add a little more water.

Slice the potatoes into a roomy bowl, sprinkle the chives and parsley over, and add enough dressing to thoroughly coat (but not drown) the potatoes, turning them gently.

Baked new potatoes & new crop garlic

serves 2

❖ Use larger, slightly older new potatoes for this dish; the really early ones are too small and waxy.

⅔ cup white wine

2 to 3 tablespoons extra-virgin olive oil

1 pound medium new potatoes, peeled and halved

1 head of new-crop garlic, cloves peeled and halved

2 or 3 bay leaves, torn

salt and freshly ground pepper

Preheat the oven to 310°F. Put the wine into a lidded, heavy cooking pot in which you will cook the potatoes (packed in fairly tightly). Bring to a boil and ignite. Once the flames have dissipated, add the olive oil and potatoes and then tuck in the garlic and bay, here and there. Season and bring to a simmer.

Put on the lid and bake in the oven for at least 1 hour, or until the potatoes are very tender.

Mum's potato cakes

serves 4, for tea

◇ We kept seconds of these warm in front of a roaring coal fire in our house. And it was always the same glass Pyrex dish that was used for cold and dark, wintry Sunday afternoon potato cakes. I'm not sure, now, whether they would taste quite the same if dished up out of anything else. I can still see the remains of liquid, golden butter glimpsed through the glass, the fire's glowing embers reflected upon its molten surface.

1¼ to 1½ pounds waxy potatoes, peeled and cut into chunks

salt and freshly ground white pepper

about ¾ cup all-purpose flour

vegetable oil

plenty of butter, to serve

Warm the oven in advance and put an ovenproof serving dish inside to warm up. Steam (for preference) or boil the potatoes in salted water until tender. If boiled, drain well and dry out in the pan over low heat for a few minutes.

Tip the cooked potatoes into a roomy pan, then immediately mash until fluffy, but not super-smooth by any means. Tip out onto a counter or tray and allow to cool and dry out for about half an hour.

Once they are ready to handle, sprinkle the potatoes with salt and grind the pepper over them. Now, little by little, sift the flour over, working it into the potatoes with your fingers, using a gentle kneading movement, until the mixture is workable but with a slight trace of stickiness. You will almost certainly need the full ¾ cup of flour, maybe a little more.

Roll out to about ⅝ inch thick and then cut into cakes the size of small cookies. Take a skillet, add a little oil, and gently heat. Dust each cake with a little flour and begin to fry them, 3 or 4 at a time. Do this ever gently until pale golden, about 3 minutes on each side. Slide them directly into the warmed serving dish and put it back into the oven to keep the potato cakes warm while you finish cooking the rest.

Once they are all cooked, cut slices of butter directly from the package and place one upon each potato cake. By the time you serve them, the butter will have reached that perfect state of half-melted. You will need a small plate, a fork, and big napkins.

Potato pie with Beaufort cheese

serves 4

A most luxurious and rich dish, which is essentially nothing more than potatoes in pastry.

1 pound medium waxy potatoes, washed

salt and freshly ground pepper

⅓ cup heavy cream

2 garlic cloves, lightly bruised

2 tablespoons butter

13-ounce package ready-made puff pastry, in 2 equal sheets

3 ounces (scant) Beaufort cheese, very thinly sliced

½ teaspoon thyme leaves

beaten egg, to glaze the pastry

Preheat the oven to 400°F. Steam (for preference) or boil the potatoes in salted water until tender, then drain, cool, and peel. Slice moderately thickly and put to one side.

Place the cream in a saucepan with the garlic, bring to a boil, then take off the heat, cover, and leave to infuse.

Put a flat baking sheet into the oven. Lightly smear another one with some of the butter. Roll out one puff pastry sheet thinly, to an ⅛-inch thickness, and lay it on the buttered baking sheet. Mark a circle on it, about 8 inches in diameter. Cover the pastry round with half of the potatoes, arranging them in a slightly overlapping layer within the circle. Lightly season and cover with half the cheese and thyme leaves, adding a few flecks of butter. Repeat these layers. Brush the pastry edges with beaten egg.

Roll out the other sheet of pastry as above and then place it over the filling. Clamp down the edges with your fingers and then trim to a round, using a tart pan ring that is slightly larger than 8 inches as a guide.

Now, brush the pastry all over with egg and, using the tines of a fork, decorate the edge. Make a small hole in the center of the pie, about ¼ inch in diameter. Remove the garlic from the cream and, using a small funnel, slowly pour the infused cream into the pie through the hole, allowing it to settle inside before adding more. Once it is quite clear that no more cream will fit, stop pouring; you may have a little left.

Slide the pie into the oven, onto the preheated baking sheet. Bake for about 20 minutes, then turn the oven setting down to 350°F. Continue cooking for another 20 minutes, or until crisp and nicely puffed; if the pie is browning too quickly, cover loosely with a sheet of foil.

Let the pie stand for a good 10 minutes out of the oven before serving. Cut into wedges and eat with a crisp green salad or just on its own.

Endive & Watercress

I have often wondered whether everyone experiences difficulty with eating bitter salad leaves until they are, at least, into their late teens—or even a touch older. They are possibly an acquired taste at any time of life, but as with cooked spinach, once adolescence is behind one, these astringent notes have a tendency to creep up and delight the taste buds.

Too many times have I told the story of being almost force-fed endive and its relatives by Chef, when an apprentice teenage cook, but the occasion was certainly a watershed moment for me. It didn't mean that I suddenly wanted to search out bagfuls of endive every single day after that, but the seeds of a lifelong love of the stuff had, most definitely, been sown.

My earliest preference was for cooked Belgian endive (or chicory, as we British call it; the Belgians themselves—or at least the Flemish Belgians—call it witloof) and remains so. I read many recipes for the cooking or braising of endive and it seems to me that those who have chosen to enlighten the reader would have it that they enjoy the vegetable a touch *al dente.* Well,

this is hardly the point; either the endive is well cooked right through until soft, or it is eaten raw. Both undeniably delicious. But to dither between the two is just silly.

The finest watercress I have eaten was in Dublin, of all places. The good folk of that fair city might well admonish me for that declaration of surprise, but it is simply that I wasn't expecting it. The unpretentious restaurant that offered it to me was a very good operation and given to serving generous portions at kind prices, but the quality of those bright and bountiful leaves was nothing short of shocking. Truthfully, I had never seen or tasted watercress like it.

The size of each sprig, so perfectly trimmed and picked over, was double—or maybe even treble—the dimensions of perfectly serviceable, English watercress from Hampshire, maybe. Combined with slivers of roast chicken, shallots, and a very fine vinaigrette, these verdant leaves made a delightful composition. Assuming all is still well at this genial establishment, it is called The Mermaid Café and is located at 69/70 Dame Street, Dublin 2.

Watercress & turnip soup

serves 4

Two slightly bitter ingredients, which surprisingly, when cooked together seem to cancel each other out, resulting in a soup of sweet subtlety.

3 tablespoons butter

6 ounces leeks, white part only, sliced and washed

½ pound turnips, peeled and diced

2 or 3 bunches (10 ounces) of watercress, washed and coarsely chopped

2 cups stock

a little grated nutmeg

salt and freshly ground pepper

1 cup milk

⅓ cup whipping cream

Melt the butter in a roomy pot, add the leeks, and cook gently until softened. Tip in the turnips, stir around for a few minutes, put on the lid, and allow the two vegetables to quietly stew together for about 5 minutes. Uncover, stir in the watercress, and let it wilt into the leeks and turnips.

Pour in the stock, lightly season with nutmeg, salt, and pepper, then bring up to a gentle simmer and replace the lid. Cook for about 20 minutes, or until the turnips are very tender. Stir in the milk and bring back to a simmer.

Check the seasoning and then purée the soup in a blender until smooth. Pass through a fine strainer, stir in the cream, and gently reheat. Particularly nice with some tiny, buttery croutons.

Watercress & curly endive salad with croutons

serves 4, generously

The bitterness of endive and the peppery qualities of watercress might, you think, argue with one another. But no, the pairing produces a harmonious assembly.

½ stale baguette

2 heads curly endive (frisée)

2 bunches of watercress, sprigs picked, washed

for the dressing

1 tablespoon red wine vinegar

2 tablespoons hot water

2 garlic cloves, peeled and crushed to a paste

salt and freshly ground pepper

4 tablespoons walnut oil

3 to 4 tablespoons olive oil

Cut 2 or 3 handfuls of croutons from the baguette and lay them out on a wire rack to dry out further.

Trim the curly endive of all outer, dark green leaves, wash well, and pat dry with paper towels.

To make the dressing, put the vinegar, hot water, garlic, salt, and plenty of pepper into a large salad bowl. Whisk together to dissolve the salt, add the oils, and continue whisking until the dressing is loosely emulsified.

To assemble, tip the croutons into the dressing and deftly mix together with salad servers, coating them well. Allow some of the dressing to soak in for a moment or two, then add the endive and watercress. Mix everything together thoroughly, lifting the croutons up through the leaves, and serve at once.

Gratin of endive with mustard sauce

serves 4 as a first course, or 2 as a light supper dish

◇ "Rich," I believe, might be the word here.

8 small, or 4 large heads of Belgian endive

3 tablespoons butter

salt and freshly ground pepper

juice of ½ lemon

⅔ cup dry vermouth

2 teaspoons Pernod (optional)

½ cup stock

⅔ cup heavy cream

2 teaspoons smooth Dijon mustard

1 tablespoon fine, fresh white bread crumbs

1 tablespoon freshly grated Parmesan

Trim the endives of any damaged leaves and remove the conical core from the base of each with a sharp knife. Melt the butter in a shallow pan and cook until foaming. Put in the endives, turning them thoroughly in the butter, and season lightly. Turn the heat down to low and gently color the endives on all sides until glossy and pale golden.

Add the lemon juice, vermouth, and Pernod, if using, and bring up to a simmer. Allow to bubble away until the liquid has reduced by about half, then turn the endives over and add the stock. Continue simmering, uncovered, for another 30 to 40 minutes, or until the endives are tender when pierced with a sharp knife at the thickest point. Remove the endives to a gratin dish and keep warm. Heat the broiler to medium.

Simmer the juices until syrupy and well flavored, then stir in the cream. Whisk together, simmer until lightly thickened, and then whisk in the mustard. Pour over the endives, coating them well with the sauce.

Mix together the bread crumbs and Parmesan, carefully sprinkle over the length of each endive, and slide under the lowest part of the broiler, to gently gild. Serve at once, perhaps with some crusty baguette to mop up the delicious sauce.

Wilted radicchio with green sauce

serves 2

◆ Try to find the long variety of radicchio, rather than the more familiar—but more readily available, it must be said—round ones. This, more than anything else, is for the look of the thing, but I think they have a better, bitter flavor, and are more fleshy, too. Note that this dish needs to be started the day before you wish to eat it.

3 large heads of radicchio, about 1½ pounds

2 cups water

⅔ cup red wine vinegar

2 teaspoons Maldon sea salt

1 very small onion, peeled and thinly sliced into rings

1 to 2 tablespoons extra-virgin olive oil

freshly ground pepper

for the green sauce

small bunch of parsley, leaves only

10 basil leaves

10 mint leaves

1 garlic clove, peeled and crushed

2 teaspoons Dijon mustard

2 teaspoons capers, drained and squeezed of excess vinegar

½ cup extra-virgin olive oil

to serve

2 hard-boiled eggs, sliced

salt and freshly ground pepper

Cut the radicchio heads vertically into quarters, through the root. Bring the water to a boil in a saucepan with the vinegar and salt added. Taking 3 or 4 quarters of radicchio at a time, plunge them into the boiling liquid for a minute or two, then drain in a colander and lay out on a dish towel to dry for a few minutes.

Lay the radicchio in a dish, scatter the onion over, spoon the olive oil over, and grind on some pepper. Gently mix together, cover, and leave in the refrigerator overnight. When you wish to serve the radicchio, remove it from the refrigerator a good hour beforehand.

To make the green sauce, put the herbs, garlic, mustard, and capers into a small food processor with 2 to 3 tablespoons of the extra-virgin olive oil. Process for a few seconds, until the solids are only coarsely chopped, and then slowly add the rest of the oil in a thin stream until the sauce is thick-ish and very green, but loose of texture and almost more like a dressing.

Arrange the radicchio and sliced eggs on serving plates and sprinkle with salt and pepper. Spoon the green sauce alongside and serve with plenty of warm, crusty baguette.

121

Spinach & Sorrel

There are two timely ways of preparing spinach, which sit at either end of its cooking spectrum and yet are equally delectable. The first—involving minimal contact with hot butter and stir-frying—is as brief as can be, whereas the second—slow stewing—almost reduces the spinach to rags. Some would say that the latter has been horribly overcooked, especially if they have only ever tasted the former, but I think they would be wrong, here.

Brasserie Lipp, on the Boulevard Saint-Germain, in Paris, offers a slowly roasted—almost braised, in fact—dish of veal known as a *fricandeau*, for a delicious Sunday lunchtime *plat du jour*. There are two choices of accompaniment to the dish: *epinards* or *lasagnettes*. Well, I have never eaten the *lasagnettes* (presumably some buttery folds of slightly more diminutive sheets of pasta than the usual lasagna), plumping always for the *epinards*, ever since the first time I tasted it well over twenty years ago. And the dish has possibly been offered, chez Lipp, for double or even triple that time, so little does the menu change at this venerable institution.

Even I was surprised when this olive-colored slop arrived in its white oval dish, looking as if it had simply been emptied out of some ancient can. But the flavor, the flavor! Much butter had clearly been used in its preparation, together with judicious seasoning including a healthy rasp of nutmeg. Occasionally on these Sundays, when not indulging in an appetizer (which is rare, for me), I ask for seconds of both the veal and the spinach, which are always gladly given, albeit with a winsome shrug.

I have often wondered whether this Lipp way with spinach is related to an extraordinary recipe in Elizabeth David's *French Country Cooking*, called *Les Epinards du Chanoine Chévrier*. The spinach leaves are finely chopped and cooked over a period of 5 days! Amounts of butter are added each day, resulting in a copious "$10\frac{1}{2}$ oz of butter incorporated . . ." by the time the dish is finally ready. Even if you find that amount of fat added to "at least 2 to 3lb of (uncooked) spinach" deeply shocking and dangerously unhealthful, you should at least try the recipe once. It is both unusual and wildly delicious.

And so to lovely sorrel. I never understand quite why this sharp and tender summer leaf/herb is not more widely available, in season. It collapses and reduces even more swiftly than spinach when cooked, transforming to a muddy green in an instant, yet its mildly acidic flavor is delicate and charming. Do try the creamy sorrel soup and the equally delicious omelet (both on page 126).

Spinach mousse with Parmesan cream

serves 4

◈ Smooth and seductive. A dainty dish.

for the mousse

a little softened butter

½ pound spinach leaves

2 large eggs

1 cup heavy cream

salt and freshly ground pepper

freshly grated nutmeg

for the Parmesan cream

1 cup whipping cream

⅓ cup freshly grated Parmesan

salt and freshly ground white pepper

Preheat the oven to 350°F. Butter the base of each of four buttered dariole molds or ramekins and line with a tiny disk of waxed paper. Blanch the spinach in boiling water for 1 to 2 minutes. Drain and refresh under very cold running water, then squeeze in a dish towel until completely dry. (You should have approximately ⅔ cup cooked spinach.)

Purée the eggs and spinach in a blender until really smooth. Pour into a bowl, stir in the cream until well mixed, and season with a little salt, pepper, and nutmeg. Pour the mixture into the prepared molds, filling them to the brim.

Cover each with a circle of foil and place in a deep baking dish. Pour tap-hot water into the dish until it comes at least three-quarters of the way up the sides of the molds. Bake in the oven for 20 to 25 minutes, or until firm to the touch.

To make the Parmesan cream, pour the cream into a saucepan and whisk in a little over ¼ cup of the Parmesan. Bring to a simmer and allow to gently bubble for a few minutes, whisking occasionally. Taste the sauce and add more cheese if you think it needs it, maybe a little salt, but definitely grind in some pepper. Simmer until of a suitable coating consistency.

Once the mousses are cooked, turn them out onto warmed plates and spoon the Parmesan cream over. Serve promptly.

Iced potage Germiny

serves 4 to 6

❖ This is a light, yet creamy soup, both sharp and refreshing. Don't be upset that the sorrel quickly turns a muddy green color when cooked, as that is simply what it does.

4 cups stock

6 large egg yolks

1 cup whipping cream

salt and freshly ground white pepper

1 pound sorrel, stalks removed and well chopped

juice of ½ lemon

minced chives, to serve

Bring $3\frac{1}{2}$ cups of the stock to a boil in a roomy pan, then turn the heat down to the merest simmer. Whisk together the egg yolks and cream with some seasoning. Now, wash the whisk and start to gently move it through the stock in a circular motion. At a regular pace, whisk the stock, adding the egg and cream liaison at the same time in a thin stream.

Let the soup cook *very* gently, stirring with a wooden spoon as if making custard. But, like custard, it can easily curdle, so watch out. The result should be limpid, smooth, and the consistency of thin cream. Immediately remove from the heat and liquidize in a blender. Pour into a bowl.

Now heat the remaining $\frac{1}{2}$ cup of stock in a nonreactive or stainless steel pan. When boiling, add the sorrel and briefly cook until thoroughly wilted. Add to the soup and stir in well, together with the lemon juice. Cool and refrigerate for at least 4 hours.

Check the seasoning and ladle the soup into chilled bowls. Serve sprinkled with the chives.

Sorrel & sour cream omelet with chives

serves 1

❖ Quite delicious eaten with a simple new potato salad (see page 112).

2 tablespoons butter

generous handful of sorrel leaves, trimmed of stalks

salt and freshly ground pepper

3 large eggs

1 scant tablespoon sour cream

1 teaspoon chopped chives

Melt half the butter in a small pan, add the sorrel leaves, and season lightly. Stew until soft and turning a muddy green color, then cook briskly until almost all the moisture has been driven off. Tip onto a plate and keep warm.

Beat the eggs with the sour cream, add the chives, and season lightly. In a favorite omelet pan, heat the remaining butter until foaming and then tip in the egg mixture. Cook the omelet in the usual way and, when almost ready, spoon the stewed sorrel over, flip over, and turn onto a warmed plate.

Spinach & ricotta crêpes

serves 4

❖ Italian *crespelle*, to reveal their provenance. The amount of batter will produce a few more crêpes than needed, but it is impractical to make less. I suggest that you cook the extra crêpes and freeze them for another occasion.

for the crêpe batter

¾ cup (scant) all-purpose flour

2 large eggs

large pinch of salt

1 cup milk

3 tablespoons butter, melted and cooled until tepid, plus a little extra for cooking

for the béchamel sauce

2 cups milk

1 bay leaf

salt

4 tablespoons (½ stick) butter

¼ cup all-purpose flour

freshly ground white pepper

for the filling

1½ pounds spinach

⅓ cup fresh ricotta cheese

2 large egg yolks

⅓ cup (rounded) freshly grated Parmesan

salt and freshly ground pepper

freshly grated nutmeg, to taste

to finish

2 tablespoons freshly grated Parmesan

To make the crêpe batter, whisk the flour, eggs, salt, and half the milk together in a bowl until smooth. Add the melted butter and enough of the remaining milk to achieve a thin, light-cream consistency. Leave to stand for 30 minutes.

To make the béchamel sauce, heat the milk with the bay and a little salt. Simmer for a few minutes, then cover and set aside to infuse off the heat. In another pan, melt the butter and stir in the flour. Cook gently for a minute or two to make a roux, but on no account allow it to color. Discard the bay leaf and add the milk to the roux, vigorously whisking until smooth. Set the sauce to cook on the lowest possible heat, preferably using a heat-diffuser mat. Stir, fairly constantly, using a wooden spoon and cook for 15 to 20 minutes. The sauce will soon become silky and smooth. Add pepper, check for salt, switch off the heat, and cover with a tight-fitting lid; this helps to prevent a skin from forming. Keep warm.

Preheat the oven to 400°F. For the filling, blanch the spinach in boiling water for a couple of minutes. Drain and refresh under very cold running water. Squeeze in a dish towel until completely dry. Put the spinach, ricotta, egg yolks, Parmesan, seasoning, and nutmeg in a food processor and briefly process to a coarse purée. Spread out on a shallow tray, cover with plastic wrap, and chill for a bit, to firm up.

For the crêpes, use an 8-inch skillet. Melt a small amount of butter in the skillet and allow it to become hot and sizzling, then pour in enough batter to thinly cover the bottom of the skillet. Cook until the underside is golden, then toss or turn and cook the second side. The first crêpe is often a bit of a mess, so you will probably need to chuck it out and then start afresh. Make 8 crêpes and put on one side.

To complete the dish, place 2 tablespoonfuls of the filling on each crêpe and roll up, tucking in the ends if necessary. Lay in a lightly buttered baking dish, with space in between each one, then carefully spoon the béchamel sauce over, allowing it to fall into the gaps (this is so the crêpes will be nicely revealed, once the dish has been baked). Sprinkle the Parmesan over and bake in the oven for 30 to 35 minutes, or until bubbling well and the surface is golden and crusted. Hand around extra grated Parmesan at table, if you wish.

Beets & Turnips

One of my earliest memories of delicious food is a deep white dish of sweet and small, tender whole beets, served buried in a parsley sauce—their bleeding, ruby juices seeping out beneath their green-flecked blanket. Unusually, for me and my nostalgic memories of Mum's cooking, this particular treat, for once, was not homegrown, but eaten in an old-fashioned hotel on the banks of Windermere, in the Lake District.

This was in the days when a typical hotel Sunday lunch involved all kinds of vegetables to accompany at least three different roasts, with maybe a seasonal lake fish, too, such as the now increasingly rare Arctic char. Admittedly, there was a habit of overcooking some vegetables, such as cabbage and brussels sprouts (though I would still rather have a soft sprout than a hard green bullet). However, this was compensated for by the most wonderful roast potatoes and parsnips, both of which benefited from being overcooked to a crisp. But those beets were cooked by someone who *really knew*.

Beets and turnips—and rutabagas, too—are very much part of our winter fare (I have slipped in a rutabaga recipe here, as it is a relative, after all), and I will always adore home-cooked fresh beets, sliced while still warm and splashed with malt vinegar. The larger turnip may be peeled and mashed in exactly the same way as the rutabaga normally is, though turnips can sometimes benefit from being blanched once in boiling water, refreshed, and then boiled till tender, as traces of bitterness can occasionally be noted. Other countries, however, can turn the common turnip into something quite ingenious.

Although I had first been taken to eat Cantonese dim sum as a trainee Egon Ronay inspector in 1977, at Joy King Lau, just off London's Leicester Square, it took nearly twenty years before I was to be convinced of the delights of fried turnip cakes. I don't quite know why they had previously eluded me. In truth I had seen many Chinatown dim sum trolleys laden down with these little square slabs, ready to be fry-griddled on specially integrated, portable stove tops, but I would always refuse a serving, however pushy the waitress—and they can surely push when offering their wares. I guess there were always just too many other good things with which I wanted to stuff my face.

So it was not until Hong Kong, in 1996—when my friend Michelle Garnaut generously treated members of her family and friends to lunch at one of the city's most famously good dim sum establishments—that I finally got properly acquainted with this delicacy. Happily, this was on the day following a celebration of her 40th birthday, and with all participants fully aware that lots of good dim sum can magically cure the most severe of hangovers. This particular place also happened to excel at fried turnip cake, so a slice was gently forced upon me. It was a revelation . . . I have been an addict ever since.

Beet jelly with dill & horseradish cream

serves 4

◇ Delicately sweet and melting on the tongue. The horseradish is a nicely fiery foil, too.

1 pound (generous) beets (or 1¼ pounds if a garnish is desired)

3 cups stock

1 teaspoon superfine sugar

4 heaping teaspoons agar flakes

for the cream

3 ounces fresh horseradish, peeled

1 tablespoon sour cream

2 teaspoons sugar

a little salt

2 teaspoons lemon juice

⅔ cup whipping cream

2 teaspoons minced dill

First cook the beets. Place them, unpeeled, in a pan of simmering salted water for about 45 minutes, until tender. Drain them and let cool for about 10 minutes; then rub off the skins. (Wear rubber gloves to avoid staining your hands.) If a garnish is desired, chop one beet into tiny cubes and reserve.

Grate the beets and put them into a stainless steel pan, together with 2 cups of the stock and the sugar. Bring up to a low simmer and cook, covered, for 10 minutes.

Meanwhile, pour the remaining stock into another, smaller pan. Sprinkle the agar flakes over and allow them to slowly soak into the liquid, then warm through, stirring occasionally, until the flakes have dissolved, about 10 minutes. Pour into the beet pan and stir all together.

Now pour the mixture through a strainer set over a bowl and allow it to drip through. Do not force the mixture or it will cloud the liquid; unlike nonvegetarian gelatin, however, there will rarely be a crystal-clear set.

Now take the beet liquid and place it over a larger bowl filled with ice cubes and water. Taking a metal spoon, gently stir the liquid around until it just begins to gel—about 10 minutes, or sooner. At this point, if you wish, the extra garnish of tiny beet cubes may be folded in; but when the mixture starts to gel, it will happen quite swiftly, so be alert.

Spoon the jelly into 4 small glass tumblers (best for the look of the thing) or ramekins, but leave enough room for the horseradish cream that will sit on top. Place in the refrigerator to set for about 1 hour.

To make the cream, finely grate the horseradish—the tears, the tears! Mix with the remaining ingredients, except the dill, and leave to infuse for a few minutes, then pass through a strainer into a bowl, pressing down well to force out as much flavor from the horseradish as possible. Stir in the dill and check for seasoning; it should be nicely nose-cleansingly hot.

Once the jellies have set, spoon a layer of horseradish cream on top and serve. Eat slowly with teaspoons, savoring every mouthful. I like to eat this entirely on its own.

Rutabaga & potato cakes with black pepper cream sauce

serves 4

❖ The addition of agar flakes is an option here, to help firm up a mixture that can veer toward wetness. However, if you can achieve a thorough drying out of the cooked vegetables, agar flakes should not be necessary.

1 pound rutabagas

10 ounces potatoes

2 scant tablespoons butter

1 teaspoon Maldon sea salt

2 teaspoons agar flakes (optional)

1 large egg yolk

1 tablespoon freshly grated Parmesan

1 tablespoon chopped scallion

flour for coating

olive oil for frying

for the sauce

1 cup heavy cream

2 teaspoons black peppercorns, cracked or coarsely crushed

salt, to taste

2 tablespoons butter

2 teaspoons smooth Dijon mustard

to garnish (optional)

watercress sprigs

Preheat the oven to 310°F. Peel the rutabaga and potatoes and cut them into chunks. Melt the butter in a lidded, roomy pot over low heat and add the rutabaga, potatoes, and salt. Stir together and gently cook for about 5 minutes; more than anything else, this is to coat the vegetables with butter and to get the pot hot. Put on the lid, transfer to the oven, and cook for about 45 minutes to 1 hour until the vegetables are tender.

Now return the pot to very low heat on top of the stove and stir the vegetables around to try to rid them of excess moisture; it does not matter if they color very slightly, or if they break up a little, either. Mash the vegetables coarsely (an old-fashioned manual masher is best, here); and, if you are uncertain about wetness, now is the time to sprinkle the agar flakes over and mix them in. Tip into a bowl and allow to cool completely before mixing in the egg yolk, Parmesan, and scallion. Spread on a flat tray and put in the refrigerator to firm up.

Meanwhile, make the simple sauce. Whisk all the ingredients together in a small pan and bring to a simmer. Cook until slightly thickened and pour into a hot pitcher or sauceboat.

Form the rutabaga and potato mixture into 8 small cakes and roll in flour to coat all over. Heat a little olive oil in a skillet and gently fry the cakes on both sides until golden; drain on paper towels.

Serve garnished with sprightly sprigs of chilled watercress, if desired, handing the sauce around separately.

Turnip gratin with cream cheese & Parmesan

serves 2

Really a lighter version of gratin dauphinois . . . made with turnips.

1 garlic clove, peeled
and crushed

½ cup (scant) heavy cream

⅔ cup milk

3 thyme sprigs

½ pound small turnips

¼ cup cream cheese

a little softened butter

1 tablespoon freshly grated
Parmesan

Preheat the oven to 350°F. Put the garlic, cream, milk, and thyme into a saucepan and bring to a simmer. Switch off the heat, cover, and allow the flavorings to infuse for 5 minutes. Meanwhile, peel the turnips and thinly slice them, preferably on a mandolin.

Strain the creamy milk through a strainer into a bowl and then whisk in the cream cheese. Tip in the sliced turnips and mix well—hands, to be frank, are best, here—while also separating the turnip slices from each other.

Lightly butter a presentable baking dish and tip in the turnips and cream, scraping out every last scrap with a spatula. Smooth over the surface and sprinkle with Parmesan. Slide into the oven and bake for 40 to 50 minutes, turning down the temperature to 310°F toward the end of cooking if the surface is coloring too much; a sheet of foil loosely tented over the dish can help, too.

Leave the gratin to stand for 10 minutes before eating. A judiciously dressed, simple green salad on the side is appropriate here.

Asian fried turnip paste

serves 4

✧ Those familiar with turnip paste will know that it contains such ingredients as Chinese dried shrimp and bacon; once fried, it is also very enjoyable with a finishing slick of oyster sauce. I decided that I ought to be able to fashion a vegetarian version, even though traditional aficionados might be horrified by such a thought. I urge you to try it—my guinea pig gourmet chums simply couldn't get enough. Although a lengthy and slightly complicated recipe, it is well worth the effort.

Naturally, Chinese cooks use their familiar long daikon, but our turnips work just fine, too. And I experimented with both! You will need sesame paste (see page 173) on hand; also some ginger syrup (see page 94)—or you could use the syrup from a jar of preserved stem ginger.

1¼ pounds turnips, peeled

1 cup water

1 heaping teaspoon Maldon sea salt

⅓ cup dried porcini mushrooms

6 scallions, trimmed

1 large green chili, seeded (for less heat) if preferred

1 large red chili, seeded (for less heat) if preferred

2 garlic cloves, peeled

⅔ cup canned water chestnuts, drained

1 rounded tablespoon peeled and finely grated fresh ginger

2 teaspoons sesame paste (see page 173)

1 tablespoon ginger syrup (see page 94)

¼ cup Chinese rice wine

¾ cup rice flour (an Asian brand, if possible, but not the glutinous variety)

2 to 3 tablespoons sesame oil

to serve

soy sauce

cilantro sprigs

First grate the turnips (a food processor is the easiest way). Place in a pan, add the water and salt, and stir together. Bring to a simmer, cover, and cook for about 30 minutes, or until the grated turnip is very tender indeed—almost a mushy consistency.

Tip the turnips and liquid into a strainer set over a bowl and press down on the turnip using the back of a ladle to extract as much flavor and juice as possible. Drop the porcini mushrooms into this liquid and leave to soak for about 15 minutes, until soft. In the meantime, mince the scallions, chilis, garlic, and water chestnuts (pulse in a small food processor for convenience).

Once soft, drain the porcini, reserving the liquid, and mince. Tip into a bowl and add the minceded ingredients, ginger, sesame paste, and ginger syrup. Mix together well.

Pour the rice wine into a measuring pitcher and add 1 cup of the reserved turnip/porcini liquid. Whisk the rice flour into this and then stir in the vegetable mixture.

Oil a small rectangular container (a small loaf pan or Tupperware box) with the sesame oil. Spoon in the turnip mixture, spreading it evenly. Cover with foil and put into a steamer. Steam over simmering water for 1½ hours, or until set and firm to the touch.

Take the container out of the steamer and remove the foil. After about 15 minutes, press a sheet of plastic wrap over the surface of the turnip paste. Allow to cool completely and then refrigerate for at least 3 to 4 hours or, even better, overnight.

Remove from the refrigerator and run a little hot water onto the sides of the mold to loosen the cake. Turn the turnip cake out onto a cutting board and cut into slices, about ½ inch thick, using a sharp knife dipped into a pitcher of boiled water.

Run a little sesame oil into a nonstick skillet and place over medium heat. Lay the slices in the skillet and fry on both sides until a rich, dark brown color; I like a few burned spots, too. Place on a heated serving platter, drizzle over some soy sauce, and add the cilantro sprigs.

Zucchini & Squash

When I had access to my neighbor (and landlord) Tessa's zucchini for the entire summer, in that hot, hot, and dry year of 1976, they became one of the daily vegetables for my little restaurant on the Pembrokeshire coast.

The zucchini seemed almost inexhaustible, and I was happily able to cut the evening's supply at about 6:30 p.m., every single day. I vaguely recall that Tessa charged me 5p (less than 5 cents) per pound—and there were a few yellow ones, too, which really shocked some of my Welsh guests, who had never seen such a thing!

Come to think about it, I would not have been surprised if many of these guests had never seen a green one, either. In the mid-seventies, in Fishguard, finding something as simple as a tube of tomato paste was an adventure in itself. "We've got ketchup, will that do?" was a common answer to the weary question.

Not really knowing, then, at the relatively tender age of twenty-two years, quite how many diverse dishes I could muster with my bounty, I simply boiled thick slices of them for a minute or two in fiercely boiling, salted water, for each table, to order, then drained them and added a large piece of butter, together with a healthy grind of pepper. And, you know, those zucchini truly didn't need anything more than that.

Since the first table's serving had still been on the plant only forty-five minutes before, the taste of them was astonishingly fine and fresh. In fact, the customers often asked for seconds and I cheerfully complied: free food, happy diner.

However hard I tried to keep track of the fast growth of my little patch, there would always suddenly appear, almost surreptitiously, a huge, lurking squash beneath the giant leaves. Knowing perfectly well that this would not be the last time this oversight occurred, I would store it and wait patiently for the next discovery, thereby having enough to prepare my mother's deliciously bland recipe for squash in white sauce, to serve with tasty roast legs of Welsh lamb for a traditional Sunday lunch.

I know that friends of mine don't see the point of cooking large summer squash at all—particularly the younger cooks of today, who seem to veer only toward dishes that must offer intense flavors and exciting textures. Well, be that as it may. When carefully steamed chunks of tender, pale green squash—and it is, to be sure, the most beautiful, pale green—are judiciously covered with a fine layer of smooth, white sauce scented with bay, clove, and nutmeg, it is a dish of great class.

And, furthermore, if then baked in the oven with a sprinkling of grated cheese (Lancashire is good), it becomes one that is fit for a king.

Piquant zucchini with sour cream & dill

serves 2

◈ A comforting and sloppy dish for Sunday supper, perhaps topped with a poached egg.

Although the paprika here is used only as a garnish at the end, it must be of good quality and freshly purchased. A good Hungarian brand would be ideal; otherwise use Spanish pimentón, but preferably not the very smoky variety.

1½ to ¾ pounds large zucchini, trimmed and coarsely grated

salt

2 tablespoons butter

1 onion, peeled and thinly sliced

freshly ground white pepper

½ cup (scant) roughly chopped dill pickles

2 teaspoons white wine vinegar

1 tablespoon chopped dill, plus extra to garnish

1 teaspoon superfine sugar

4 tablespoons sour cream

a sprinkling of paprika, to garnish

Sprinkle the grated zucchini with salt, only to season them, not more. Put them to drain in a colander with a dish underneath. Leave for 1 hour, then, using your hands, squeeze out the excess liquid. Put the zucchini to one side.

Melt the butter in a heavy cooking pot. Add the onion and stew until soft, but not colored. Tip in the zucchini and stir them around with the onion until well mixed. Grind a little pepper over, put on the lid, and cook very gently for about 5 to 7 minutes, stirring occasionally.

Using a blender, purée the dill pickles with the vinegar, dill, and sugar.

Remove the lid from the zucchini, turn up the heat, and, if necessary, drive off any excess liquid. Add the purée, stir in the sour cream, and bring the mixture up to a simmer. Cook for a few more minutes until the assembly is thick and unctuous. Check for seasoning.

Turn into a heated serving dish or divide between individual shallow soup bowls. Sprinkle with extra chopped dill and generously sprinkle with paprika.

Zucchini timbale with pimento dressing

serves 4

◇ If I may humbly say, a carefully considered vegetarian option.

1 pound zucchini, trimmed and coarsely grated

1 teaspoon salt

1 rounded tablespoon butter

freshly ground white pepper

2 large eggs

1 large egg yolk

¾ cup (rounded) sour cream

2 heaped teaspoons finely grated Parmesan

2 teaspoons minced dill

2 teaspoons minced chives

the merest scrap of garlic, minced

a little softened butter

for the pimento dressing

1 small garlic clove, peeled and minced

salt and freshly ground pepper

1 teaspoon sherry vinegar

1 teaspoon Dijon mustard

5 tablespoons good olive oil

1 tablespoon boiling water

few shakes of Tabasco

½ cup (rounded) bell roasted peppers (from a jar), minced

Mix the grated zucchini with the salt, put to drain in a colander, and leave for 1 hour. Squeeze thoroughly dry in a dish towel.

Preheat the oven to 300°F. Melt the butter in a roomy skillet and add the zucchini with some pepper. Cook gently for 10 minutes or so. Allow them to become lightly gilded, but also try to make sure that any excess moisture produced is driven off by the heat. Tip onto a plate to cool.

Put the eggs, egg yolk, sour cream, Parmesan, herbs, and garlic into a roomy bowl and mix to combine, but do not overbeat; if this "custard" is too light and airy, it will puff too much while cooking and then, unattractively, sink back. Stir the cooled zucchini into the custard and correct the seasoning.

Generously butter 4 ramekins, place a tiny circle of waxed paper in the bottom of each, and fill to the brim with the mixture. Stand them in a deep roasting pan and add boiling water to come at least two-thirds of the way up the sides of the ramekins. Bake for about 30 minutes, or until just firm to the touch.

Meanwhile, prepare the dressing. Whisk the garlic, seasoning, and vinegar together in a bowl to dissolve the salt. Now whisk in the mustard, olive oil, water, and Tabasco. Finally, stir in the roasted bell peppers.

Remove the ramekins from the water bath and leave to cool slightly for about 10 minutes. Run a small, sharp knife around the edges of the custards and then carefully turn out onto serving plates. Pour the sauce over or around to suit yourself. Best eaten warm.

Summer squash & tomato masala

serves 4

❖ This wonderfully aromatic dish is unusually delicious. Large summer squash, being the bland but texturally soothing vegetable it is, throws out much liquid as it cooks. Here, together with juices from the tomatoes—as they pop and burst in the heat of the assembly—it produces a dish that would not seem out of place on a stall in the streets of Mumbai, perhaps ladled out of some giant tin cauldron. In fact, so copious are the juices generated here, it is almost a chunky broth.

If you don't want to eat the skin of the squash, simply scoop off the flesh with a spoon and leave the skin behind. However, if the squash is fresh and young, this should not be necessary. Do try to find curry leaves, however, as they do add to the aroma of the thing.

1 large summer squash, about 2 pounds

salt

2 onions, peeled and thinly sliced

2 garlic cloves, peeled and sliced

2 tablespoons vegetable oil

1 tablespoon masala paste (see page 55)

about 12 curry leaves, fresh or dried (optional)

1½ pounds ripe, red cherry, or baby plum tomatoes

3 tablespoons butter, thinly sliced

freshly ground pepper

Preheat the oven to 310°F. Trim the ends of the squash, cut it in half down through the middle, and then halve each piece lengthwise. Scrape out the fiber and seeds with a teaspoon and then cut each quarter in half yet again, also lengthwise, giving 8 squash "boats."

Sprinkle salt generously over all cut surfaces and place the squash in a colander. Leave for about 40 minutes to leach out a little of the juices. Rinse and dry in a dish towel.

Meanwhile, in a large, lidded pot, fry the onions and garlic in the oil until golden. Add the masala paste and stir around for a few minutes. Lay the squash pieces, skin side down, on top and add the curry leaves (if using), then tip the tomatoes over. Season and dot with the slices of butter. Cover and place in the oven to cook for about 1½ hours.

Delicately decant into deep soup plates, so each one has two pieces of squash, a spoonful of the tomatoes, and plenty of aromatic broth.

Mushrooms Tame & Wild

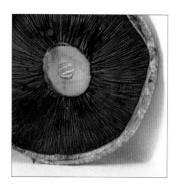

Although I think I may have mentioned this before, it seems that the common or garden white mushroom has all but disappeared from the menu of most British restaurants. It is almost as if the chef doesn't think it quite good enough, an embarrassment to his good taste and exotic sensibilities.

Well, I can only see this as a great shame, for there is nothing nicer, as far as I am concerned, than, say, a summery dish of diminutive white mushrooms cooked *à la grecque*, or a trio of large and dark, open-cap fellows baked *en persillade* with a golden, bread crumbed crust. And then, of course, there is a simple, smooth-as-silk cream of mushroom soup garnished with tiny, buttery croutons—and also very good served chilled, in summer.

No, these days, it seems that all mushroom dishes, or those that include them, must be wild, or at least dried wild, or cultivated fungi such as shiitake, oyster, and those miniature, spooky and stringlike enoki (*Flammulina velutipes*, as I'm sure you know), which are a particular favorite of the cook who thinks he or she is inclined toward the Asian school. And, ironically, the regular use of these wild and faux-wild fungi on restaurant menus partly contributed toward the title of this book.

Alongside goat cheese, sun-dried (or oven-roasted) tomatoes, arugula, and, occasionally, eggplants, it is to the wild mushroom that chefs prefer to turn when faced with the "vegetarian option" for that day's lunch menu. I also reckon that this task is often given to the lowliest chef in the kitchen, as the other cooks are far too busy getting ready to "froth" and "foam" all kinds of sauce and emulsion.

Ergo, it is out with the pasta or rice and into a bowl of warm water with a handful of wrinkly dried fungi. That is not to say that the resultant dish might not be quite delicious, but I never understand why someone does not, just occasionally, cook some sliced white mushrooms with shallots, dry vermouth, a little cream, and, say, some chopped tarragon, then pile them onto a slice of buttered toast or, even better, onto a slice of crisp, fried bread. Serve with a simple green salad, and there is as delicious an option as

I can think of. But there are always exceptions: fresh morels cooked in cream, for instance.

If you are lucky enough to either forage fresh native morels in the spring or find a greengrocer or upscale market that will stock them, then this is something special indeed. For best results, I find it quite unnecessary to fry them first, though most chefs will. Rather, after first rinsing and drying them in a dish towel, I add them directly to a pan with a clove of garlic crushed to a paste with salt, some pepper, and a small piece of butter, then pour on enough whipping cream just to cover them. I let them stew gently until the cream has noticeably thickened, the morels softening but retaining a pleasing sponginess (taste one), then stir in a spoonful of chopped chives and a squeeze of lemon juice.

Eat this just as it is, or on toast or, if very hungry, stirred into some freshly cooked pasta. The rare wild mushroom not, for once, just an option, but the absolute reason for eating astonishingly good food.

Persillade of porcini & potatoes

serves 2

✧ There is something especially aromatic and magical that occurs when parsley and garlic are finely hand chopped together. Apart from anything else, the smell is intoxicating, as the juices mingle together under the blows from a heavy blade. I promise you that the end result, once heat is applied, would not be quite the same if the two were prepared separately.

2 medium, waxy potatoes, peeled

4 to 6 medium to large porcini (fresh or frozen), cleaned

large handful of Italian parsley leaves

2 garlic cloves, peeled

3 to 4 tablespoons olive oil

salt and freshly ground pepper

Finely shred the potatoes (the shredder attachment of a food processor is ideal), then wash in a strainer under cold running water until the water is clear. Drain and dry well in a dish towel. Thinly slice the porcini. Finely chop the parsley and garlic together by hand.

Heat 2 tablespoons of the olive oil in a large skillet (preferably nonstick) and quickly fry the porcini with a little seasoning, until lightly colored. Remove to a plate with a slotted spoon. Add another 1 tablespoon oil to the pan and sauté the potatoes with a little seasoning until beginning to color. Reintroduce the porcini and mingle with the parsley and garlic. Toss together over brisk heat until smelling quite wonderful. Eat without delay.

Mushroom salad with Parmesan vinaigrette

serves 2

✧ As simple and savory as can be, and all the better for that.

¾ pound firm, white or closed cap mushrooms

juice of ½ lemon

1 scant tablespoon white wine vinegar

2 tablespoons warm water

salt and freshly ground white pepper

1 very small garlic clove, peeled and crushed

1 to 2 tablespoons freshly grated Parmesan

2 to 3 tablespoons extra-virgin olive oil

2 tablespoons whipping cream

1 very small shallot, peeled and minced

plenty of minced parsley

Thinly slice the mushrooms and place in a shallow dish suitable for serving. Squeeze the lemon juice over and stir together. Put to one side.

Blitz the vinegar, water, and seasoning together in a small food processor for a second or two to dissolve the salt, then introduce the garlic, 1 tablespoon of the Parmesan, and the olive oil. Blend to homogenize the mixture, then add the cream and give a final quick blitz; do not overprocess at this stage for fear of curdling the cream.

Pour the dressing over the mushrooms, gently mix together, and then neaten the arrangement for serving. Finally, sprinkle the shallot, parsley, and remaining Parmesan on top, to taste. Eat with slices of warm and buttered, crusty baguette.

Mushroom consommé

serves 4

◈ This is delicious supped with Rachel Cooke's wonderful Parmesan crackers (see page 214) on the side, but perhaps cut into fingers, rather than circles, so more closely resembling a cheese sablé.

If you are serving the consommé hot, you may like to add an extra splash of Madeira. Or if serving cold, carefully float a spoonful or two of lightly whipped whipping cream—flavored with some minced tarragon leaves and scantily acidulated with tarragon vinegar—upon the surface of the consommé.

2 large onions, about ¾ pound, peeled and thickly sliced

3 to 4 tablespoons olive oil

1½ pounds flat, dark–gilled mushrooms, thinly sliced

3 garlic cloves, peeled and crushed

salt and freshly ground pepper

½ cup dry vermouth

6 cups stock

for the clarification

½ pound flat, dark–gilled mushrooms, sliced

¾ cup chopped celery

3 or 4 tarragon sprigs

1 tablespoon tarragon vinegar

3 large egg whites

⅓ cup Madeira

Using a large pot, very slowly fry the onions in 2 to 3 tablespoons of the olive oil until a rich, golden brown color; this will take 30 minutes or so. Remove with a slotted spoon to a plate and reserve.

Now put the mushrooms in the pot, with a little more oil if necessary, and also cook until golden brown. Add the garlic and seasoning, turn up the heat, and stir-fry for a couple of minutes. Add the vermouth and allow to bubble vigorously. Reintroduce the reserved, cooked onions and then pour in the stock. Cover and simmer gently for 40 minutes. Strain the broth into a clean pan, leave to settle, and then remove any fat with paper towels, briefly laid upon the surface. Allow to cool.

For the clarification, blitz together all the ingredients in a food processor until fairly smooth. Whisk the mixture into the mushroom broth and slowly bring up to a simmer, stirring until it is becoming quite hot. Now leave the broth to gently bubble under what will be a raft of mushroom mush, floating on the surface; check that this is fully floating, as you do not wish for any solids sitting on the bottom of the pan, which will burn. Allow the liquid to continue blipping its way through the raft for about 30 minutes.

Strain the broth through a strainer lined with a double-folded sheet of cheese-cloth or a fine, linen dish towel. Leave to drip through this to reveal—hopefully – a crystal-clear consommé beneath. Serve hot, or chilled in summertime.

Gratin of stuffed mushrooms

serves 4

❖ Sunday supper?

8 large, flat mushrooms, with deep interiors for stuffing

3 tablespoons butter

1 onion, peeled and minced

1 large celery stalk, peeled and minced

salt and freshly ground pepper

grated zest and juice of 1 large lemon

1¼ cups fresh white bread crumbs

2 hard-boiled eggs, grated

2 tablespoons chopped parsley

1 teaspoon thyme leaves

2 garlic cloves, peeled and minced

2 tablespoons olive oil

8 tablespoons heavy cream

1 to 2 tablespoons freshly grated Gruyère

lemon wedges, to serve (optional)

Preheat the oven to 350°F. Remove the stalks from the mushrooms and set the caps to one side; mince the stalks.

Melt the butter in a deep skillet and fry the onion, celery, and chopped mushroom stalks with a little salt and pepper until pale golden. Tip into a bowl and add the lemon zest, bread crumbs, eggs, parsley, thyme, and garlic. Mix thoroughly with a fork and try not to compact the mix. Put to one side.

Heat the olive oil in a solid-bottomed baking dish—one that will happily transfer from cooktop to oven. Slide in the mushroom caps, open side down; they should fit snugly. Lightly season and allow the mushrooms to gently sizzle on the burner, then turn them over. Remove from the heat and squeeze the lemon juice over.

Now fill each mushroom cap with some of the stuffing mixture, but do not pat it down. Bake in the oven for 25 to 30 minutes, turning the oven down slightly if the stuffing is browning too much.

Turn the oven setting up to 400°F. Using a small knife, check to see that the mushrooms are tender, then pour a spoonful of cream over each one. Lightly sprinkle with the Gruyère and return to the top shelf of the oven. Continue to cook until the cream is bubbling and the cheese lightly gilded.

Serve the mushrooms at once, with extra lemon squeezed over if desired. Delicious eaten with a simply dressed watercress salad.

Parsley, Sage, Rosemary & Thyme

The one particular drawback of living in a second floor flat in West London is that of lacking enough space to grow herbs. I guess I wouldn't really want a garden unless it was in the countryside, but enough essential herbs growing seasonally all year round would be a veritable boon.

I would like a bushy bay tree, for one. Similarly, a rosemary bush. Hardy thymes, too, and sage, of course. Then I could indulge in masses of basil, one or two varieties of mint, both types of parsley, chives, and the deliciously delicate chervil. Tarragon (the French, obviously, rather than the tasteless impostor, the weedlike Russian) would be near the top of the list, too. Oh that I could!

I have an outdoor windowsill that will accommodate a couple of boxes, which I am happy to fill with favorites during the summer: garden mint, mainly, and some basil plants for the shorter, hotter periods. But that is it, really. Parsley might just be there, too, but one recipe demanding a big presence would surely end its short life in one cutting. I adore lots of parsley around me, so am resigned to purchasing it.

Bay, I filch with permission from Father Huw Chiplin, my local vicar, who has a convenient front garden to his vicarage, which I regularly pass on my way to the corner shop. There he has four—four!—healthy bay trees behind his wall, and, armed with my trusty kitchen scissors, I snip, snip, snip my way along his bushes, fussily, collecting only the largest branches with the largest leaves. These I then dry in the kitchen and thank the Lord, and his employee, for such generous gifts. Huw's bushes really are particularly fragrant, I must say, and easily comparable with some filched leaves (without permission, I am now embarrassed to say) from a side street in sunny Beaulieu, in the South of France on another occasion.

These days, fresh herbs are vital to my cooking, but this was not always the case. It is now so very easy to forget a time when such luxuries—and yes, they are, don't forget—were simply an unthinkable asset to the kitchen of the keen home cook. Moreover, even during my apprenticeship in a French restaurant in the North of England, an occasional bunch of fresh tarragon in a brown paper bag would travel up to Manchester by train from London, tucked among other essentials: Bayonne ham, dried wild mushrooms (morels, cèpes, chanterelles), preserved truffles, and walnut oil.

Very occasionally, a few of these fresh leaves would be chopped up to further enhance a béarnaise sauce, then scented with a reduction involving some powdery dried leaves, though as fine as these could be. But, generally, the entire leafy offering would be plunged into a large jar of vinegar to, ironically, then flavor it for use in a reduction for—you've guessed it—more béarnaise sauce. Hey ho!

For once, we really must thank the supermarkets—and greengrocers and farmers' markets—for their abundance of fresh herbs, to enhance our cooking each and every day. Remember, once upon a time, the only parsley one might come home with—freely, granted—was a few sprigs wrapped up with a pound of Friday cod fillet.

Parsley, radish & celery salad with capers

serves 2

Simple, fragrant, sharp, and crisp. Make sure the salad ingredients are cold before assembly.

small bunch of Italian
parsley, leaves only,
roughly torn

7 or 8 long French radishes,
trimmed and quartered

1 shallot, peeled and very
finely sliced into rings

3 small celery stalks, taken
from the heart, cut into
sticks

2 teaspoons capers,
together with 2 teaspoons
of their vinegar

squeeze of lemon juice

salt and freshly ground
pepper

2 tablespoons extra-virgin
olive oil

Mix everything together in a large bowl and turn out onto a serving dish.
Eat with buttered slices of warmed baguette.

Lima beans with sage, olive oil & dried chili

serves 4, generously

◈ If you prefer an even spicier flavor, you might like to use half olive oil and half chili oil.

2 cups dried lima beans

3 cups water or stock

1 whole head of garlic, sliced in half across its middle

3 or 4 sage sprigs

3 or 4 small, dried red chilis

4 to 5 tablespoons olive oil

salt

Put the beans into a large saucepan, cover with plenty of water (not the given amount), and bring to a boil. Switch off the heat, cover, and leave for 1 hour. Drain and rinse in a colander under cold running water.

Preheat the oven to 310°F. Put the beans into a lidded, solid pot and cover with the 3 cups water or stock. Slowly bring to a simmer and skim off any scum that forms on the surface. Add all the other ingredients except the salt and stir. Put on the lid and bake in the oven for about 1 hour, until the beans are tender. Only now add salt to taste; added at the beginning of the cooking process, it will toughen the skins.

Ladle into shallow soup plates and serve warm, rather than piping hot. A sprinkling of fine vinegar would, for me, make the beans even nicer.

Roasted shallots with rosemary

serves 4

◈ I am loath to suggest adding salt to this recipe, as once the stock used has reduced, there should be enough. You can always add a touch more at the end, if necessary.

2 tablespoons olive oil

2 scant tablespoons butter

24 large shallots, peeled (but not the extra-large type)

scant sprinkling of sugar

freshly ground white pepper

4 tablespoons white wine vinegar

⅓ cup stock

several bushy rosemary sprigs

Preheat the oven to 375°F. Heat the olive oil and butter in a solid and shallow, cooktop-to-oven casserole (a Le Creuset would be ideal here). Once hot, add the shallots and gently fry, turning them regularly, until lightly colored all over. Sprinkle with the sugar and pepper and pour in the wine vinegar. Allow the vinegar to bubble away to almost nothing and then pour in the stock.

Bring up to a boil, tuck in the rosemary sprigs, and put into the oven. Bake for 40 minutes or so, turning the shallots over once, until soft and well burnished and the stock has reduced to a sticky juice. Serve directly from the dish.

Thyme, onion & Gruyère tart

serves 4 to 6

❖ Very savory indeed and so lovely and luxurious, too.

for the pie crust

4½ tablespoons (generous ½ stick) cold butter, cut into cubes

¾ cup all-purpose flour

pinch of salt

1 to 2 tablespoons ice water

for the filling

3 tablespoons butter

1½ pounds white onions, peeled and very thinly sliced

1 large egg

2 large egg yolks

¾ cup heavy cream

2 teaspoons Dijon mustard

1 teaspoon thyme leaves

salt and freshly ground white pepper

½ cup freshly grated Gruyère

freshly grated nutmeg

To make the pie crust, briefly process the butter, flour, and salt together in a food processor until the mixture resembles fine bread crumbs. Now tip into a large, bowl and gently mix in the water with cool hands or a table knife, until well amalgamated. Knead the dough lightly, then put into a plastic bag and refrigerate for at least 1 hour before rolling.

For the filling, melt the butter in a wide, shallow pan. Tip in the onions and very gently sweat over moderate heat for at least 40 minutes, or as long as 1 hour, until pale golden and completely soft. Cool.

Meanwhile, preheat the oven to 350°F, and place a flat baking sheet inside to heat (it will help the base of the tart to cook thoroughly).

Roll out the pie crust on a lightly floured counter as thinly as you dare, then use to line an 8-inch, 1¼-inch-deep tart pan. Prick the base with a fork. Line the pie crust with foil and dried beans, slide onto the hot baking sheet, and bake "blind" for about 15 to 20 minutes. Remove the foil and beans and return the pie crust to the oven for another 10 minutes or so, until it is golden, crisp, and well cooked through, particularly the base.

Mix together the egg, egg yolks, cream, mustard, and thyme leaves. Carefully mix in the onions, season, and pile the mixture into the pie crust. Sprinkle the Gruyère over the surface and generously grate some nutmeg on top. Bake in the oven for about 45 minutes, or until the filling is a rich golden color and just firm to the touch. Leave to stand for 10 minutes before eating.

Potato pancakes with sour cream & chives

serves 4

To make clarified butter, melt a stick of unsalted butter in a small pan until there is froth on the surface and a milky residue on the bottom. Remove the froth with a spoon and discard, then ladle out the clear butter into a container, leaving the milky residue behind. You may not need to use all the clarified butter here, but it keeps well in the refrigerator, covered, for a few weeks.

The milky residue can be used in the pancake batter—fill up with milk to give the ¼ cup required. Waste not, want not, I always say.

for the pancake batter

1 to 1¼ pounds potatoes, peeled and cut into large chunks

¼ cup (scant) milk

2½ tablespoons all–purpose flour

3 large eggs

4 large egg whites

2½ tablespoons heavy cream

salt and freshly ground pepper

clarified butter for frying (see above)

for the sour cream and chives

⅔ cup sour cream

2 tablespoons chopped chives

large pinch of cayenne pepper

pinch of salt

Warm the oven to low in advance and put a large ovenproof plate inside to warm up. Steam the potatoes until cooked, or boil carefully and allow to dry out in the warm oven. While still hot, put them through a food mill or a potato ricer; do not use a food processor or the potato will become gluey. Allow to cool slightly in a mixing bowl. Now beat in the milk, flour, eggs, egg whites, cream, and seasoning.

For the sour cream and chives, mix everything together in a bowl and adjust the seasoning if you need to.

Heat a little of the clarified butter in a heavy-bottomed skillet or on a cast-iron flat griddle pan. You will need to cook the pancakes in batches: pour 3 or 4 small ladlefuls of the batter onto the surface of the skillet, spacing them apart. Moderate to high heat is called for here; you need a slight sizzle and a light browning at the edges of the pancake after about 2 minutes.

The time to turn over is when the tiniest bubbles appear on the uncooked surface. Take a spatula and quickly flip the pancake over. The cooked surface should be perfectly mottled with pale brown blisters and have a thin golden ring around the edge.

Finish cooking for another minute or so. The texture should be slightly springy but feel moist. As you cook the pancakes, keep them warm in the oven on the plate, covered with foil.

Hand around the pancakes and the sour cream and chives separately, so that each person may pop a dollop onto each pancake. Very delicious.

Chilled curried mint & cucumber soup

serves 4

❖ Another way one can fashion this soup is to reduce the curry powder to 1 to 2 teaspoons. Once the soup has cooled to tepid, whisk in 2 tablespoons of the green paste (below), or to taste. Delicious . . .

2 small cucumbers

salt and freshly ground white pepper

1½ tablespoons butter

1 small onion, peeled and chopped

1 tablespoon curry powder

1 cup (scant) stock

1 small sweet apple, peeled, cored, and chopped

⅔ cup (scant) plain yogurt

⅔ cup (scant) coconut milk

⅓ cup whipping cream

2 tablespoons chopped mint

juice of 1 small lime

1 small, hot green chili, seeded and chopped (optional)

Peel the cucumbers, cut in half lengthwise, and scoop the seeds out, using a teaspoon; reserve the skin and seeds. Finely dice the cucumber flesh, mix with a little salt, and place in a colander to drain for 30 minutes or so.

Meanwhile, melt the butter in a saucepan and fry the onion until soft. Stir in the curry powder and cook together for a few more minutes, then add the stock and chopped apple. Simmer for about 20 minutes, or until the apple is very tender. Let cool.

Once cooled, purée the soup with the yogurt, coconut milk, and the reserved cucumber debris (seeds, skins, etc.) using a blender, until very smooth indeed. Pass through a fine strainer into a bowl and then stir in the cream. Season with salt and pepper to taste.

Briefly rinse the diced cucumber and squeeze lightly to remove excess liquid. Stir into the soup with the mint, lime juice, and, if desired, the green chili. Cover and chill in the refrigerator for at least 2 hours before serving, in chilled soup bowls.

Green paste

to fill 2 small tubs

❖ This wonderful, spicy, and fragrant condiment is utilized in other recipes in the book, such as the samosas (on page 64). Store it in the refrigerator and its color will remain green for 2 or 3 days, or pack into small, lidded plastic tubs and freeze—to keep it fresh and green for longer.

7 to 10 hot or mild green chilis, to taste

9 cups cilantro leaves

4 cups mint leaves

8 garlic cloves, peeled

2 teaspoons ground cumin

1 teaspoon sugar

1 heaping teaspoon sea salt

⅓ cup lime juice

¼ cup unsweetened shredded coconut

¼ cup coconut milk

Seed the chilis or not, depending on your heat threshold. Place in a small food processor, together with all the other ingredients, and blitz to make a smooth purée. Scrape out into lidded plastic containers and put into the refrigerator.

Soupe au pistou

serves 6

◈ Nice in Nice and nice anywhere, anyway.

½ pound leeks, trimmed, thinly sliced, and washed

¾ cup peeled and chopped celery

2 tablespoons olive oil

½ pound potatoes, peeled and diced

1 cup (rounded) peeled and diced eggplant

1½ cups trimmed and diced zucchini

5 to 6 cups water

2 teaspoons Maldon sea salt

3 cups chopped collard greens or green cabbage

3 cups washed and chopped spinach or chard leaves

approx. 1 thumb's thickness (1¾ ounces) spaghetti, broken into short lengths

¼ pound green beans, trimmed and cut into ¾–inch pieces

2½ cups canned haricot (navy) beans, drained and rinsed

freshly ground white pepper

for the pistou

⅓ cup extra–virgin olive oil

large bunch of basil

3 garlic cloves, peeled and crushed

3 tablespoons freshly grated pecorino or Parmesan cheese

In a large pan or cooking pot, gently stew the leeks and celery in the olive oil until softened. Tip in the potatoes, eggplant, and zucchini, then pour in the water and add the salt. Bring up to a simmer and cook for 10 minutes.

Now stir in the collard greens, spinach, and spaghetti. Cook for another 10 minutes, then stir in the green beans, haricot beans, and pepper. Bring the soup up to a final, gentle simmer and continue cooking for another 20 to 30 minutes, or until all is very soft, thick, and a nice dull-ish green color—as it should be.

For the pistou, simply purée all the ingredients together using a small food processor; or, if you are an artisan pistou maker, employ a mortar and pestle.

I like to eat this soup almost at room temperature, or at least warm rather than piping hot, with the pistou handed around separately, so that each person can add as little or as much as they like.

Macaroni & Cannelloni

Unlike many of my peers, when I was still cooking in a restaurant kitchen, the fabrication of homemade pasta was never very high on my list of special food. As near perfect pastry as we could achieve, yes. The smoothest and most freshly churned ice creams and sorbets, yes. The highest risen, crisp-and-yet-soft-inside and cooked to order Yorkshire puddings for Sunday lunch, most definitely. But rolling out sheets of fresh pasta, well, no, not really. Nothing against it at all, it is just that I think there are other cooks—Italians, obviously—who, quite simply, make it much better. They have an affinity with it. The making of pasta is in their blood.

Since leaving the professional role, I now do, occasionally, enjoy dusting off the pasta machine to roll out lovely thin sheets of yellow pasta for the making of ravioli—as you will realize from the butternut squash ravioli (on page 43), which are very simply formed. There is no stamping out with little fluted cutters or some such, they are simply folded over into raggedy little square-ish packages. For me, the most important part of the operation is to take the pasta to the machine's finest setting, so achieving the ultimate, delicate wrapper. This will also help when pressing together the edges of the ravioli, which are, in effect, now double the thickness and must be squeezed between the fingertips to make them as thin as possible. Failure to do this can result in a tough and doughy edge.

Personally, if cooking regular pasta at home —spaghetti, tagliatelle, linguine, that kind of thing—I will always prefer to use a fine quality dried brand. Cipriani egg pasta is my particular favorite and usually carries the additional qualification of being *extra sotilli* ("extra thin"). It is a beautiful product, priced accordingly, but never disappoints. If you cannot find Cipriani pasta (it is mostly available in specialty food shops and Italian delis, and, occasionally, super-markets), then I would recommend De Cecco.

One of the most gorgeous pasta dishes of my life is the one that Franco Taruschio used to make when he and his wife, Ann, were at The Walnut Tree, near Abergavenny, in Wales. The dish was called Vincisgrassi and involved alternating layers of lasagna, sliced porcini, thin slices of prosciutto crudo, béchamel, and Parmesan. And if truffles were in season, these would be shaved over each piping-hot—and I mean, piping—serving, just after emerging from the oven.

I have successfully made a vegetarian version of this wonderful dish by, obviously, leaving out the ham and, instead, substituting briefly cooked spinach, refreshed in iced water, squeezed of excess moisture, and then distributed as pretty green strata between the pasta and porcini. If porcini are unavailable, then sliced flat mushrooms are a most serviceable alternative— if not with quite so heady an aroma.

Macaroni &cheese with tomatoes

serves 2

◈ Self explanatory, really, when all is said and done.

1¾ cups milk

1 bay leaf

freshly grated nutmeg

salt and freshly ground white pepper

3 tablespoons butter

2 tablespoons all–purpose flour

¾ cup (rounded) sharp Cheddar, grated

1½ cups macaroni

4 small, ripe tomatoes, thinly sliced

1 tablespoon freshly grated Parmesan

To make the cheese sauce, heat the milk with the bay, nutmeg, and a little salt. Simmer for a few minutes, then take off the heat, cover, and allow the flavors to mingle for 10 minutes. Preheat the oven to 350°F.

In another pan, melt the butter and stir in the flour. Cook gently for a minute or two to make a roux, but on no account allow it to color. Remove the bay leaf, add the milk to the roux, and vigorously whisk together until smooth.

Set the sauce to cook on the lowest possible heat (preferably using a heat–diffuser mat) and stir, fairly constantly, using a wooden spoon. The consistency will soon become silky and unctuous. After about 10 to 15 minutes, stir in the cheese, then add pepper and taste for salt. Cook for another 3 to 4 minutes. Switch off the heat and cover with a tight-fitting lid; this helps to prevent a skin from forming. Keep warm, nearby.

Add the macaroni to a pan of lightly salted boiling water and boil until tender, then drain very well. Mix with the cheese sauce and spoon into a lightly buttered baking dish. Cover with the tomatoes, slightly overlapping the slices, and sprinkle evenly with the Parmesan.

Bake in the oven for about 30 to 40 minutes, until the tomatoes are lightly blistered and the edges are bubbling up nicely from underneath.

Mushroom cannelloni

serves 4

◈ I know it seems odd that I have chosen to use a can of tomato soup here, but I really like the flavor it gives to the sauce for this particular dish. My reasoning is that some time ago, for cannelloni, I used a carton of Spanish-made tomato sauce, which was very smooth and thick, but also had a flavor similar to the canned soup. All who tasted it thought it was terrific—and had no idea it had come from a carton. As the Spanish sauce is not available to all, this method attempts to replicate it.

for the thick tomato sauce

2 garlic cloves, peeled and crushed

3 tablespoons butter, plus a little extra for the dish

1¾ cups canned chopped tomatoes

1 x 10–ounce can cream of tomato soup

for the cannelloni filling

1 onion, peeled and chopped

2 garlic cloves, peeled and chopped

2 tablespoons butter

½ pound flat mushrooms, roughly chopped

salt and freshly ground pepper

2 or 3 tarragon sprigs

2 or 3 parsley sprigs

juice of ½ lemon

big splash of dry vermouth

for the béchamel sauce

2 cups milk

1 bay leaf

freshly grated nutmeg

4 tablespoons (½ stick) butter

¼ cup all-purpose flour

to assemble

8 cannelloni tubes (ideally De Cecco brand)

2 to 3 heaping tablespoons freshly grated Parmesan

Lightly butter a large, shallow, ovenproof baking dish that will easily hold 8 cannelloni tubes, with space in between each one.

For the thick tomato sauce, in a saucepan, stew the garlic in the butter until pale golden. Add the tomatoes with very little salt and the canned soup. Gently simmer until reduced by almost two-thirds; the sauce should be very thick. Pass it through a strainer directly into the baking dish, spreading it around with a spoon until level. Put to one side.

For the cannelloni filling, fry the onion and garlic in the butter to soften. Add the mushrooms, season, and stew until all is soft and fragrant. Meanwhile, strip the leaves from the herb sprigs and mince them. Add the herbs, lemon juice, and vermouth to the pan; turn up the heat and cook until almost dry. Leave to cool, then blitz in a food processor until somewhere between coarse and fine. Preheat the oven to 350°F.

To make the béchamel sauce, heat the milk with the bay, nutmeg, and a little salt. Simmer for a few minutes, then cover and allow the flavors to mingle for 10 minutes. In another pan, melt the butter and stir in the flour. Cook gently for a minute or two to make a roux, but do not allow it to color. Take out the bay leaf, add the milk, and whisk vigorously until smooth. On the lowest possible heat (preferably using a heat-diffuser mat), set the sauce to cook for about 15 to 20 minutes, stirring fairly constantly, using a wooden spoon. The sauce will soon become silky and unctuous. Add pepper, check for salt, switch off the heat, and cover with a tight-fitting lid; this helps to prevent a skin from forming. Keep warm.

Once the mixture has cooled, fully fill the cannelloni tubes with it (I find a pastry bag is the most efficient way). Lay them side by side in the dish, pushing them into the tomato sauce. Make sure all is neat and then blanket with the béchamel sauce. Shake the dish a little to settle everything and sprinkle the entire surface with Parmesan. Bake for 40 to 50 minutes, until all is bubbling and well crusted.

Spaghetti al aglio & peperoncino

serves 2

◈ I love the way the sticky, golden garlic behaves when cooking with the chili and oil here. The smell is heavenly, too!

6 garlic cloves, peeled and sliced

2 large red chilis, thinly sliced

4 to 5 tablespoons extra-virgin olive oil

handful approx. 1¼ inches in diameter (7 ounces) dried spaghetti

salt

Cook the garlic and chilis very gently in a small pan with the olive oil, until the garlic (the *aglio*) is pale golden and both are crisp. Lift out with a slotted spoon and put onto a small plate; reserve the oil.

Cook the spaghetti in a large pan of salted boiling water until *al dente*. Drain well in a colander and rinse with warm water.

Now take a large skillet (preferably nonstick) and add some of the flavored oil. Heat gently and then tip in the spaghetti. Turn and toss the pasta around until well coated with oil. Add the chili and garlic and toss until well dispersed.

Turn the spaghetti onto two very hot plates, adding a little extra oil if you think it necessary. Eat without delay.

Tagliatelle with scarlet runner beans, basil & mint

serves 4, as a light lunch or supper

◈ I like the mimicry here between the strands of pasta and the sliced beans.

1 pound scarlet runner beans or Romano beans, trimmed

2 tablespoons butter

1¼ cups whipping cream

5 ounces soft cream cheese

1 large garlic clove, peeled and minced

½ teaspoon Maldon sea salt

freshly ground white pepper

generous grating of nutmeg

⅓ cup freshly grated Parmesan, plus extra for serving

¾ pound Cipriani tagliatelle, or other fine–quality egg tagliatelle or fettuccine

2 handfuls of basil leaves

handful of mint leaves

Thinly slice the beans lengthwise, removing the outer stringy sides.

Put the butter, cream, cream cheese, garlic, seasoning, nutmeg, and Parmesan into a medium pan and slowly bring to a simmer, gently whisking at the same time to melt everything together. Put to one side.

Have a large bowl of ice water ready. Add the beans to a large pan of generously salted boiling water and cook until just tender. Lift them out in batches with a large slotted spoon and immediately immerse them in the ice water, dispersing them with your hands to cool them down as swiftly as possible. Don't discard the cooking water.

Once the beans are really cold, tip them into a large colander and drain thoroughly. Return them to the (now empty) bowl and stand it in the sink.

Now, making sure that there aren't any stray bits of cooked bean in the reserved cooking water, bring it back to a boil. Add the pasta and cook until *al dente*. Carefully balance the colander over the beans in the bowl and drain the pasta over them; this will, effectively, reheat the beans at the same time.

Lift out the colander, shaking out any clinging water from the draining pasta, and place on the draining board. Lift the bowl of beans in hot water out of the sink. Replace the pasta colander in the sink and drain the beans over the pasta. Toss and shake the beans and pasta together using a couple of large forks, or salad servers, until evenly combined.

Coarsely chop the basil and mint leaves together, stir them into the reserved cream mixture, and warm through. Pour into the pan in which the pasta was boiled and then add the pasta and beans. Over very gentle heat, carefully lift and turn them through the cream and herb mixture until well coated and hot.

Serve on warmed plates and hand around freshly grated Parmesan at table.

Gnocchi alla Romana

serves 4, generously

◈ This may not be the best known of gnocchi recipes, but it is a reassuringly comforting one. It is lovely eaten entirely on its own, or with tomato sauce (see page 19 or 164).

4 cups milk

1 cup (generous) semolina

1¼ cups freshly grated Parmesan

7 tablespoons (1 scant stick) unsalted butter, cut into cubes

2 large egg yolks

1 rounded teaspoon Maldon sea salt

freshly ground white pepper

freshly grated nutmeg

In a roomy, heavy-bottomed pan, bring the milk to a boil. Now, whisking constantly, pour in the semolina in a steady stream. Continue to whisk until it is thoroughly mixed in, without any lumps. Turn the heat to very low, exchange the whisk for a stout wooden spoon, and continue cooking and stirring for another 10 minutes, or so, until really thick.

Take off the heat and quickly beat in half the Parmesan and half the butter with the egg yolks, salt, pepper, and nutmeg until well blended and smooth. Spray a flat baking tray lightly with water. Using a spatula dipped into hot water, spread the mixture out evenly on the tray, to a thickness of about ½ inch. Leave to cool completely.

Preheat the oven to 425°F. Lightly butter a large, oval baking dish. Using a 1½-inch cookie cutter, cut the cold paste into circles (a small dish of warm water on hand, in which to occasionally dip the cutter for a neat cut, is useful).

Lay the gnocchi slightly overlapping in the baking dish, dot with the remaining butter, and sprinkle with the rest of the cheese. Bake on an upper (but not topmost) shelf in the oven for about 15 to 20 minutes, until the gnocchi are nicely gilded and sizzling; a final quick flash under the broiler can also be employed, if necessary.

Pappardelle with artichokes and sage

serves 2

❖ As simple and delicious as can be. If at all possible, use the Cipriani brand of pappardelle, which is packaged in a swish-looking, dark blue box and available online.

8 small artichokes

juice of 1 small lemon

2 to 3 tablespoons extra-virgin olive oil

2 garlic cloves, peeled and thinly sliced

6 or 7 sage leaves, roughly chopped

salt and freshly ground pepper

5 ounces pappardelle

freshly grated Parmesan

Trim the outer leaves from the artichokes, slice off their tops, and then slice thinly, discarding any choke. Immediately toss with the lemon juice.

In a nonstick skillet, heat 2 tablespoons of the olive oil and gently fry the sliced artichokes until beginning to take on a pale golden color. Add the garlic and sage and cook for a few more minutes until the garlic is lightly colored too. Season well and keep warm.

Cook the pappardelle in a large pan of lightly salted boiling water until *al dente*. Place a serving bowl in the sink and suspend a colander over it. Tip the pasta into the colander to drain; the boiling water will warm the bowl. Lift the colander, discard the water, and tip the pasta into the bowl.

Toss the pasta with a little more olive oil. Add the artichokes and mix together. Serve on hot plates and hand around some Parmesan at table.

Split Peas & Chickpeas

At the Diwana Bhel Poori House, behind London's Euston Station, there is a daily vegetarian lunchtime buffet offered of such breadth, quality, and value that I wonder why I don't venture there more often. There is almost every kind of legume imaginable—assorted lentil dishes, sharply spiced and dressed bowls of chickpeas, soupy dhals, and various beans. Together with a colorful array of green vegetable dishes, potatoes, and roots, it is, to be sure, a vegetarian heaven. Note, particularly, a dish piled high with dark green *methi*, the slightly bitter fenugreek leaf, so fragrantly delicious.

Here, in Britain, I feel we have never been interested enough in legumes (or pulses, as we call them) to make of them anything more than sustenance. In the Northeast, there is the "pease pudding," of course. To make it, typically, yellow split peas are cooked in stock until very soft indeed, then beaten to a paste; an egg is added and then the mixture is either baked in the oven or wrapped in cheesecloth and boiled, until set firm. It may be eaten hot or cold, but either way, it is usually thickly sliced. I guess it is okay when

served with the traditional ham it is often cooked with, but as a dish in its own right—and with all due respect to the proud cooks of that region—well, I remain a touch unconvinced.

Most people's relationship with the chickpea now appears in the shape of a supermarket plastic pot of hummus. I don't decry this at all, being an occasional purchaser myself, but it bears no relationship whatsoever to the exquisitely fine pastes prepared in the kitchens of very good Lebanese and Middle Eastern restaurants, where a more correct amount—more generous, in fact—of tahini (sesame paste) is incorporated.

Even more importantly, for me, at least, is the amazing super-smooth consistency they manage to achieve. I am further captivated by its traditional presentation: in a small, deep terracotta dish and smoothed up the sides to form a well, which is filled with good olive oil, a little cayenne/paprika, and chopped parsley. Hot pita bread and lemons are the only accompaniments necessary. The hummus served at Al Waha, in Westbourne Grove, West London, is one of the very best I have eaten.

Greek fava

serves 2 to 3

❖ In Greek, *fava* refers to a spread made from yellow split peas. I first ate this when I was staying with some English friends in their house in the Peloponnese. It is very comforting and delicious when eaten spread onto toasted pita bread. Although I think it is not traditional, I like to add garlic to the fava, too. If you are able to find pale pink, mild, and sweet-fleshed onions (often in Asian food stores), please use these.

Most would say that it is not necessary to soak split peas these days. Well, not being most people, I do soak them; I find they cook more evenly and, as a result, turn out tender and soft.

1 cup yellow split peas, soaked overnight or for at least 6 hours in cold water

4 cups water

2 medium pink (or red) onions, peeled—1 coarsely chopped, 1 finely sliced

4 garlic cloves, peeled and coarsely chopped

3½ tablespoons extra–virgin olive oil, plus a little extra to serve

salt and freshly ground pepper

1 lemon, quartered

Drain the soaked peas, place them in a cooking pot or heavy-bottomed pan, and pour on the 4 cups water. Add the chopped onion, garlic, and olive oil. Do not add any salt, for now. Bring up to a boil, skim off any scum that rises, and simmer uncovered for about 1½ hours, adding salt only after the first hour. The peas must be very well cooked and turned almost to mush, without too much excess water; if necessary, drain some off.

Pass it all through the coarse blade of a food mill, rather than use a food processor, which will purée the mixture too much.

Pour the fava into a warmed serving dish. Spoon over some more olive oil, scatter with the sliced onion, and grind over plenty of pepper. Best eaten warm. Serve with cut lemons to squeeze over it.

Simply dressed hearts of romaine lettuce would be an accompaniment with contrast, but I prefer to eat this just with toasted pita.

Warm chickpea salad with sesame dressing

serves 2

❖ This salad is absolutely *made* by the inclusion of my sesame paste (see below), which also appears in several other recipes. Make sure the canned chickpeas are of good pedigree—ideally a Greek or Middle Eastern brand. Also, if the olives are packed in oil, use this for the dressing.

2½ cups canned chickpeas

for the dressing

2 teaspoons sesame seeds

2 ripe tomatoes

1 garlic clove, peeled and minced

2 scallions, trimmed and finely sliced

2 teaspoons red wine vinegar

2 tablespoons olive oil

1 tablespoon sesame paste

1 tablespoon each chopped Italian parsley and mint

1 heaping tablespoon chopped black olives

For the dressing, lightly toast the sesame seeds in a dry pan over medium heat until fragrant, and cool slightly. Peel, seed, and chop the tomatoes and mix together with the rest of the dressing ingredients in a roomy bowl.

Tip the chickpeas into a pan, bring to a simmer, and heat briefly for a few minutes. Drain in a strainer and rinse with boiled water from the kettle.

Add the hot chickpeas to the dressing, stir together, and serve, spooned over slices of toasted sourdough or country bread, if you like.

Sesame paste

makes about 1¾ cups

❖ You need a powerful, small food processor to make this paste. For the best flavor, I feel it is important to use Asian brands of chili and sesame oils.

⅔ cup sesame seeds

3 tablespoons finely grated ginger (juice saved!)

1 large garlic clove, peeled

2 tablespoons light soy sauce

4 tablespoons mirin (Japanese cooking wine)

1 to 2 tablespoons chili oil

⅓ to ½ cup sesame oil, plus a little extra to serve

2 tablespoons lemon juice

½ cup warm water

1 to 2 tablespoons sugar, to taste

Lightly toast the sesame seeds in a dry pan over medium heat until fragrant, and cool slightly. Tip into a small food processor and add all the other ingredients. Grind and pulse until you have a paste that is fully emulsified and super-smooth.

Pour into two small, lidded containers, smooth the surface, and trickle over a little extra sesame oil, to preserve the surface. Put in the refrigerator, where the paste will keep happily for anything up to 1 month. Or you could freeze one of them, if you like.

Green lentil salad with piquant vegetable vinaigrette

serves 4 as a first course or accompaniment, or 2 as a hearty main dish

❖ It is just about possible to chop the solid ingredients together in a food processor, but hand-prepared will give a more even texture; food processors have a habit of missing some bits.

1½ cups French green (Puy) lentils, washed

2 tablespoons minced carrots

2 tablespoons minced red bell pepper

2 tablespoons minced scallion

2 garlic cloves, peeled and minced

2 tablespoons minced gherkins (use crisp cornichons)

2 tablespoons minced green olives

2 teaspoons minced capers

2 tablespoons red wine vinegar

4 to 5 tablespoons extra-virgin olive oil

salt and freshly ground pepper

3 hard-boiled large eggs, minced

2 heaping tablespoons chopped flat-leaf parsley

Cook the lentils in about 2 cups water until tender; do not add salt. Meanwhile, in a bowl, mix all the rest of the salad ingredients, except the eggs and parsley, together. Drain the lentils and allow them to cool slightly for a few minutes.

Tip the lentils into a bowl and add the vegetable vinaigrette. Stir together well, season generously, and pile onto a serving dish. Scatter the chopped eggs and parsley on top and eat warm or at room temperature.

My dhal

serves 2 to 3

◆ Depending upon how sloppy or thick you like your dhal, I have given a flexible amount of water to play with. At any time during the cooking process, more water may be added, but it is best that you use hot water from a boiled kettle—to keep the temperature even during cooking. Although it is not essential to soak the moong dhal, I think it cooks more consistently if it is presoaked.

1½ cups moong dhal, soaked overnight in cold water

1 tablespoon turmeric

4 to 6 cups water

⅓ cup oil or ghee

1 tablespoon cumin seeds

2 teaspoons black mustard seeds

1 onion, peeled and minced

4 garlic cloves, peeled, and crushed

salt and freshly ground pepper

2 large tomatoes, peeled and minced

1 small carrot, peeled and grated

1½ cups coconut milk

coarsely chopped cilantro, to finish (optional)

Drain the soaked moong dhal, place in a cooking pot or heavy-bottomed pan, add the turmeric, and pour on the 4 cups water; do not add salt. Bring to a boil and cook for about an hour until tender, adding more water as necessary (see above).

In a separate pan, heat the oil until hot. Add the cumin and mustard seeds and briefly fry until popping. Tip in the onion and garlic and fry until a rich golden color. Add to the dhal and stir in.

Season with salt and pepper to taste and then add the tomatoes, carrot, and coconut milk. Simmer all together very gently for about 20 minutes, until the carrot is thoroughly cooked through. Serve in warmed bowls, with some chopped cilantro sprinkled on top, if you like.

Baked barley "pilaf" with Provençal vegetables

serves 3 to 4

❖ A colorful, jewellike assembly with the lovely flavors of a ratatouille permeating the barley.

2¾ cups pearl barley, soaked overnight in cold water

1 large onion, peeled and minced

4 to 5 tablespoons olive oil

4 garlic cloves, peeled and minced

2 cups stock

2 bay leaves

2 teaspoons harissa (optional)

1 small eggplant, diced

1 small green bell pepper, cored, seeded, and diced

1 small red bell pepper, cored, seeded, and diced

1 medium zucchini, diced

2 large, ripe tomatoes, diced

salt and freshly ground pepper

Preheat the oven to 350°F. Drain the pearl barley, rinse in a strainer and then drain thoroughly.

Using a large, lidded cooktop-to-oven pot, fry the onion in 1 tablespoon olive oil until golden. Add the barley and garlic, with a little more olive oil, and stir around until well coated. Pour in the stock, add the bay leaves, and stir in the harissa, if using. Turn off the heat, cover, and put to one side.

Heat a little more olive oil in a large skillet (preferably nonstick) and briskly fry the eggplant, peppers, and zucchini until nicely colored. Add the tomatoes, stir around briefly, then tip all these vegetables into the stock and barley. Bring up to a simmer, put on the lid, and bake in the oven for 20 to 25 minutes. On removing from the oven, do not take off the lid. Leave for 5 minutes.

Now uncover and fluff up the pilaf with a couple of forks. Season to taste. Lay a dish towel over the top, clamp it in place with a lid, and leave for another 5 minutes, to allow any excess steam to be absorbed. Serve on hot plates.

This is delicious eaten with slices of toasted country bread, brushed with olive oil and smeared thickly with fresh garlic purée (see page 90).

White beans, porcini & cream

serves 2

◈ Make this quick dish in porcini season (late summer to late fall), when they are plentiful (in Europe and western North America). Otherwise, frozen ones can be used successfully. Reconstituted dried porcini (soaked in warm water for 20 minutes), on the other hand, will produce a good dish, but will not contain those deliciously slippery moments of fresh fungi among the soft and creamy beans.

2 shallots, peeled and minced

2 tablespoons butter

1 tablespoon dry vermouth

⅔ cup whipping cream

2 garlic cloves, peeled and minced

½ pound fresh porcini, cleaned and thinly sliced

2½ cups canned haricot (navy) or cannellini (white kidney) beans

1 heaping tablespoon chopped parsley

small squeeze of lemon juice

salt and freshly ground pepper

a little freshly grated Parmesan

Using a fairly deep pot, fry the shallots in half the butter until softened and just a little golden. Add the vermouth and allow to sizzle and reduce a little. Pour in the cream and stir in the garlic. Bring up to a simmer, switch off the heat, cover, and leave to infuse. Preheat a broiler.

In a small skillet, melt the remaining butter and gently fry the porcini until pale golden and smelling fabulous. Tip into the cream infusion and stir in. Drain the beans in a strainer and rinse with boiling water from a kettle, then shake well until dry. Add the beans, along with the parsley, lemon juice, and seasoning to the creamy porcini and heat through.

Tip into a shallow gratin dish. Sprinkle over the Parmesan—not too much, just as a savory, finishing touch. Place under the broiler to glaze for a few minutes. Serve at once, perhaps with a salad of bitter, fall leaves.

Savory corn pudding

serves 4

❖ My American friend Betsey Apple supplied me with a recipe for corn pudding. It may have changed almost beyond recognition now—so sorry, Betsey, but your recipe is the inspiration for this dish. It is delicious eaten with some very ripe tomatoes, skinned, chopped, and seasoned, mixed with sliced scallions and basil, then lubricated with a little excellent wine vinegar and olive oil.

2 very fresh ears of corn, about 1 pound in total

2 tablespoons unsalted butter, melted

1 heaping teaspoon potato flour

²⁄₃ cup (scant) milk

²⁄₃ cup (scant) heavy cream

large pinch of ground mace

1 teaspoon Maldon sea salt

freshly ground white pepper

3 large egg yolks, well beaten

1 small ball of buffalo mozzarella, drained and cut into small chunks

1 to 2 tablespoons freshly grated Parmesan, plus a little extra to serve if desired

Preheat the oven to 400°F. Cut the ears of corn in half, then stand them upright and cut the kernels from the cobs, using a sharp knife (yield: about 1 ¾ cups kernels). Melt the butter in a saucepan and stew the corn for a few minutes until almost tender.

Slake the potato flour with a little of the milk in a small bowl. Add the rest of the milk and the cream to the corn with the mace, and season with the salt and plenty of pepper. Bring up to a gentle simmer and then stir in the slaked potato flour. The mixture will thicken almost immediately, so stir together well and quickly, then remove from the heat. Leave to cool for about 5 minutes, then stir in the beaten egg yolks.

Butter a shallow, 1-quart-capacity baking dish and pour in the mixture. Scatter the chunks of mozzarella on top and then, using your fingers, push them under the surface. Sprinkle the grated Parmesan over and bake in the oven for about 30 minutes.

Lift out from the oven carefully and leave to cool slightly. Serve from the dish, spooning out onto warmed plates at the table. Sprinkle some extra Parmesan over, if desired.

Grilled white polenta with fonduta

serves 4

◇ The fontina cheese needs to be grated and soaked in the milk the night before you want to make the dish, so do this and make the polenta the day before you wish to eat it. Fonduta is closely related to Swiss fondue.

for the polenta

4 cups water

1 teaspoon salt

1 cup (rounded) white polenta

2 tablespoons unsalted butter, cubed

about ½ cup freshly grated Parmesan

a little olive oil for grilling

for the fonduta

1¾ cups coarsely grated fontina cheese (see above)

1 cup (scant) milk

5 tablespoons butter, cubed

3 large egg yolks

to serve

extra freshly grated Parmesan

To cook the polenta, first bring the water and salt to a boil in a large, heavy-bottomed pan. Take a solid whisk and begin to stir the water. With your other hand, slowly tip in the polenta in a fine, steady, sandlike stream. Do not stop whisking until all the polenta has been added. Turn down the heat to very low, or preferably place the pan on a heat-diffuser mat, and continue whisking for a few moments.

Add the butter and grated Parmesan. Change the whisk to a wooden spoon and continue stirring with this. Once the polenta starts to come away from the sides of the pan, it is ready. Pour it into an oiled, straight-sided plastic box, ideally, so that, once set, it may easily be slipped out and thickly sliced, ready for grilling. Keep in the refrigerator until ready to use.

To make the fonduta, put the (soaked) cheese and milk, and the butter in the top half of a double boiler or in a heatproof bowl. Cook over simmering water until the cheese has completely melted. Add the egg yolks one by one, beating each into the mixture until thoroughly blended in. Once incorporated, continue stirring until thickened, glossy, and just pourable.

To serve, cut the polenta into slices, about ½ inch thick. Lightly brush each surface with olive oil and heat a ridged griddle or a solid-based skillet until very hot. Grill the polenta slices until well colored on each side; this will take a good 5 minutes or so; I like it quite burnished.

Place two pieces of polenta on each warmed plate and generously spoon the fonduta over. Sprinkle with a little extra Parmesan and eat at once.

Risotto & Pilaf

Whenever I attempt to diet with a lowering of my carbohydrate intake these days, it will always be rice that I miss most. This wasn't always the case, though, for an understanding of rice cookery is a skill that came rather late to me. Before this, it was potatoes that had left the largest hole of desire, along with all things encased in delicious pastry. Pasta was always lower down this order of regime—but which is not to say that marvelous, authentically made lasagna doesn't remain one of my favorite things to both cook and eat.

All the rice cookery I used to attempt always turned out as one great big disappointment to me. There was my waterlogged plain boiled rice, a risotto with the texture of pudding, and a pudding in which the milk seemed completely alien to the rice with which it was intended to bond. Even a simple pilaf eluded me, although I had been precisely instructed by a sweet and friendly Anglo-Indian cook in my late teens. Because of all this constant failure, it further caused me to dislike eating the stuff, too. A kind of gastro-sulk had firmly set in.

So, it was not until I discovered a method of making pilaf from the exacting words of Madhur Jaffrey, and from one of her earlier books, that I eventually enjoyed some success. Apart from the fact that the amount of liquid used was far less than I had otherwise previously employed, there was also a finishing process that I was ignorant of: the absolute non-removal of the lid of the pot for several minutes after having been taken from the oven, with a further instruction of laying a dish towel over the pot once the rice had been fluffed up with a fork. I should also add that the brand of basmati rice sold under the name of "Tilda" always seems to behave better than others. And I never wash Tilda rice, either, even though this preliminary task is thought of as essential by almost everyone.

As far as risotto is concerned, I had it all wrong right from the start. In the early 1980s I was very proud of my risotto using a pre-fluffed (in other words, part-cooked rice), which bears no resemblance to the real thing, be it everyday arborio, or the specialist grains—vialone nano and carnaroli. Well, one lives and learns . . .

And, you know, hardly any of us then knew which was the correct rice or had much idea as to how authentic risottos should be made. I eventually turned to the scientifically informed and marvelous Marcella Hazan, who put me straight with her words of wisdom.

It occurs to me, in fact, that the majority of influence over the years has been that of women cookery writers. And how correctly and wonderfully sexist is that?

Tomato risotto

serves 2

◇ I have always been a stickler for the fat used in making risotto being all about butter. However, it seemed right, here, to use olive oil at the beginning of the process; I think it may have something to do with this one also being all about tomatoes, so synonymous with olive oil. Don't worry, however, there is plenty of butter to come at the end . . .

½ pound ripe cherry tomatoes, halved

2 garlic cloves, peeled and minced

pinch of dried chili flakes

salt and freshly ground pepper

1 onion, peeled and minced

1 tablespoon olive oil

1 cup (scant) carnaroli rice

1¾ to 2 cups hot stock

3 tablespoons butter

1 tablespoon dry vermouth

1 tablespoon freshly grated Parmesan, plus extra to serve

Blend the tomatoes, garlic, chili, and a little salt in a food processor to a very smooth, liquid purée. In a deep-sided, heavy-bottomed pan, fry the onion in the olive oil until softened and pale golden. Tip in the tomatoes and simmer until reduced by half. Add the rice and turn up the heat. Stirring vigorously with a sturdy wooden spoon, allow the rice to soak up the tomato and then add a ladleful of stock. Still stirring, let the rice absorb the stock before adding another ladleful. Continue adding the stock in this way; you may not need all of it.

Stop adding stock when the risotto is looking a lovely, pale orange color, is sloppily pourable, and the rice is starting to become tender and not chalky in the middle (I always keep tasting a grain as I go). Now remove from the heat and quickly beat in the butter. Cover and leave to settle for 5 minutes.

Check for seasoning and vigorously beat in the vermouth and Parmesan. Spoon onto hot plates and hand extra Parmesan around at table. For me, when spooned from its cooking pot, the perfect texture of a risotto is that of slow lava.

Buttery pilaf with two onions, coconut & green paste

serves 2

◈ It is not essential to include the green paste here, but it further perks up this already fragrant pilaf. One of my favorite dishes in this book.

1 medium onion, peeled and minced

4 tablespoons (½ stick) butter

1 cup basmati rice (preferably Tilda)

1 cup (scant) stock

½ cup coconut milk

salt and freshly ground white pepper

4 thinly pared strips of lemon zest

1 tablespoon green paste (see page 157), or 2 tablespoons chopped cilantro

2 tablespoons finely sliced scallions (mostly green parts)

juice of ½ lemon or lime

Preheat the oven to 350°F. Using a lidded, cooktop-to-oven pot, fry the onion in half the butter until a rich golden color. Add the rice, stir it around until well coated with buttery onion, and then add the stock, coconut milk, salt, plenty of pepper, and the lemon zest. Bring to a simmer, stir once to distribute everything, and pop on the lid. Bake in the oven for 15 minutes. On removing from the oven do not take off the lid! Leave to stand for 10 minutes.

Now thoroughly stir in the green paste or cilantro, scallion, and the remaining butter. Place a dish towel over the pot, tuck it down inside slightly, clamp it down with the lid and leave, once more, for another 5 minutes; this allows the rice to further steam, with the towel absorbing any excess, so resulting in a dry and fluffy pilaf. Serve on hot plates and squeeze the lemon or lime juice over it.

Congee with bok choy, golden fried garlic, green chili & soy

serves 2 for a main dish, or 4 as a first course

✧ "Asian savory rice porridge" would be a fairly accurate description, here. Also, it is one of the finest hangover foods I know, although deeply comforting at any time. For a truly authentic taste, try to find Chinese sesame oil, chili oil, and light soy sauce (a superior brand in each case).

⅔ cup jasmine rice

4 to 6 cups stock

7 thick slices fresh ginger (unpeeled)

3 tablespoons Chinese Shao-xing rice wine

for the garnishes

3 or 4 bok choy, or similar Chinese greens, steamed until tender, then sliced

4 or 5 large garlic cloves, peeled, thinly sliced, and gently fried in a little oil until pale golden and lightly crisp

2 or 3 scallions, trimmed and thinly sliced

shredded fresh ginger, steeped in rice vinegar

2 fresh, large green chilis (generally milder than red ones), sliced

to finish

light soy sauce

toasted sesame oil and/or chili oil

In a large, heavy-bottomed pot, mix together the rice, 4 cups stock, and the ginger and bring up to a simmer. Cover and cook very gently indeed (a heat-diffuser mat is helpful), for at least 1 hour or maybe longer, stirring from time to time; the desired consistency should be that of porridge, and with the rice and stock harmoniously married; you may need more stock to get it just right. As ever, practice makes perfect. (You may also prefer to cook it in a very low oven, covered, but it must be finished on the cooktop.)

Naturally, the rice will be overcooked almost to the point of submission. Once you are happy with its consistency, fish out the ginger and discard, then add the rice wine and stir in.

To finish the congee, ladle it into bowls, distribute the garnishes as you see fit, then trickle on a little of the soy and oils.

Scrambled & Baked

I remain forever amazed and perplexed—and sometimes quite cross, if the truth be known—that perfectly accomplished cooks are so capable of making a complete hash over scrambling eggs. But even more bewildering is that the same person is then also quite happy to sit down and eat them!

The sad little yellow heap is, naturally, going to be woefully overcooked, and a pale liquid (usually added milk) will have separated out from the eggs. This seepage, of course, will further soak into a slice of pale, undercooked, and flabby toast, upon which these bouncy lumps will just about tumble, but with plenty of bits skittering around the plate, too. The cooking receptacle will have been some battered old pan, which is now coated in furry yellow stuff. Someone with whom I once shared an apartment, years ago, would then leave a pan such as this to soak *for days*.

One of the main problems with managing something so inherently simple, is that the preparation is often rushed. As opposed to an omelet, which can—and should—be deftly made in a matter of seconds, scrambled eggs need the exact opposite treatment. In these more modern times since my flat-sharing days, I have discovered that it is well worth investing in a solid-based, nonstick pan.

Apart from the obvious benefits with the ease of washing it later, the nonstick coating of the pan allows a somewhat more evident observation of how the eggs are coming along as they quietly curdle into a mass, easily lifted from the bottom of the pan as the spoon nudges its way around. It goes without saying that the heat should be tentative.

The finest butter will further enhance the taste of the finest scrambled eggs, although I do not believe that adding cream improves that which is already going to be a rich assembly. Milk? Well, I am not exactly sure. My mother certainly used to beat some milk into the eggs, but I have always put that down to thrift rather than improvement.

The simplest way to prepare a dish of baked eggs is to break one large or two small eggs into a well-buttered, eared dish, season them, and spoon over a couple of tablespoonfuls of cream.

Bake for anything from 7 up to 10 minutes in the oven, at 350°F, for a runny yolk and a just-set white. Or you can cook them in a steamer, but the cooking time should be slightly less and the water beneath only at the gentlest simmer.

Practice, as usual, makes perfect, but I do tend to poke them with a tentative finger when I think they are ready, just to see if the white is setting beneath the cream and the surface of the yolk is turning opaque. If you prefer to use small ramekins—the French *oeufs en cocottes*, in other words—the accuracy of cooking the eggs becomes more difficult to judge, with the bubbling cream above disguising what is going on in this deeper vessel. However, this way has a special charm to it, with nice things happening when spooning into the depths.

Baked eggs with cream, ramps & morels

serves 2

❖ This particular egg dish celebrates that seasonal moment when ramps and fresh morels happily coincide. The first asparagus, later in the morel season, is another possible partner for baked eggs. Naturally, you should use the very freshest, most beautiful eggs you can lay your hands on. Although the quality of the other ingredients is important, it is the eggs, above all, that must shine.

3 tablespoons butter, plus extra to butter the dishes

12 small fresh morels, briefly rinsed, dried, and cut in half lengthwise

salt and freshly ground pepper

15 to 20 ramps, washed and trimmed

2 large or 4 medium, very fresh eggs

4 tablespoons heavy cream

Preheat the oven to 350°F. Lightly butter 2 shallow, ovenproof dishes. Melt slightly less than half the butter in a skillet, add the morels, season, and lightly fry until tender. Lift out with a slotted spoon and divide between the two buttered dishes.

Slice the ramps into thick ribbons. Return the pan to the heat, add the rest of the butter, and cook the ramps, also seasoned, until softened and wilted. Spoon into the dishes.

Mix the ramps together with the morels and spread toward the edges of the dishes, so making room for the incoming egg(s). Pour 1 tablespoon cream into each dish, break in the egg(s), season, and then pour on the rest of the cream. Slide into the oven and cook for 7 to 10 minutes, until cooked with a runny yolk and a just-set white. Serve at once.

Scrambled eggs & tomatoes on toast with olive oil & Parmesan

serves 2

❖ I make these quite delightful scrambled eggs by blitzing ripe cherry tomatoes—skins and cores intact—to a smooth purée. These normally offending parts become indistinguishable and do not spoil the dish in any way, trust me. If, however, you use ripe, larger tomatoes, peeling and seeding is advised. Some shredded basil leaves added at the time of scrambling can be a pleasing addition. Summer Sunday supper at its finest, I'd say, wouldn't you?

1/2 pound cherry tomatoes

1 or 2 garlic cloves—1 peeled and crushed to a paste with 1/2 teaspoon Maldon sea salt; 1 halved, to finish (optional)

pinch of dried chili flakes or freshly ground pepper

1 tablespoon extra-virgin olive oil, plus a little extra to serve

5 large eggs, beaten

2 slices country or sourdough bread

1 1/2 to 2 tablespoons freshly grated Parmesan

Blitz together the tomatoes, crushed garlic, chili or pepper, and olive oil in a blender or food processor until smooth. Place in a saucepan (preferably nonstick) and allow to reduce over moderate heat until thick and saucelike. Tip in the eggs and slowly scramble them with the tomato until done to your liking; I advise just pourable.

Meanwhile, toast the bread. You may like to lightly rub the surfaces with a cut clove of garlic, for more punch. Pile the scrambled eggs and tomatoes onto the toasted bread, sprinkle with Parmesan, and trickle a little olive oil over to serve.

Egg mayonnaise

serves 2

◈ Very fresh eggs and good, thick homemade mayonnaise are essential here.

3 large eggs (at room temperature)

several inner, pale yellow leaves of a Boston lettuce

homemade mayonnaise (see below)

small handful of watercress leaves

4 radishes, trimmed, washed and quartered lengthwise

a few chives

cayenne pepper

To cook the eggs, put them into a pan, cover with cold water, and bring to a boil, then switch off the heat, put on the lid, and leave them for 6 minutes to cook in the residual heat. Then run cold water into the pan for about 3 minutes to halt the cooking. This should achieve a perfectly cooked yolk, with a nicely set, rather than rubbery, white.

To serve, arrange the lettuce leaves on two plates. Shell the hard-boiled eggs and cut in half lengthwise. Place 3 halves on each portion of lettuce, then neatly coat with enough mayonnaise to just cover them. Scatter the watercress around the edges of the eggs and add the radishes here and there. Using kitchen scissors, snip chives over the eggs and sprinkle with cayenne pepper.

Mayonnaise

makes about 2 cups

◈ This is a good, thick mayonnaise, which keeps well in the refrigerator. It is important to have all the ingredients at room temperature before you start. Do not be frightened of adding all the oil; it will be fully incorporated if you follow the method. Also, for efficiency and ease, I recommend using an electric hand mixer.

2 large egg yolks

2 teaspoons smooth Dijon mustard

salt and freshly ground white pepper

1¼ cups sunflower or other neutral oil

juice of ½ large lemon

⅔ cup (scant) light olive oil

Place the egg yolks in a roomy bowl and mix in the mustard and a little seasoning. Beginning slowly, beat these together while very slowly trickling in the neutral oil (I always find that this will emulsify easier than olive oil, for some reason). When the mixture becomes very thick, add a little lemon juice. Continue beating, adding the oil a little faster now and speeding up the beating.

Once the neutral oil has been exhausted, add some more lemon juice and then begin incorporating the olive oil. Once this has also been used up, add a final squeeze of lemon juice. Taste for seasoning; you may also like to add a little more lemon juice, if it suits. Pack into a lidded plastic container and refrigerate until ready to use.

Oeufs mollets à l'indienne

serves 4

❖ I particularly like to serve these eggs upon a bed of rice salad with peas, so I have included the recipe here, but you can serve them on their own if you prefer. You will need to have a quantity of curry essence and some homemade mayonnaise on hand.

8 large eggs (at room temperature)

curry essence
(see page 78)

about 6 tablespoons homemade mayonnaise (see left)

8 thin strips of roasted red pepper, from a jar

for the rice and pea salad

1 cup basmati rice (preferably Tilda)

1⅓ cups water

1 heaping teaspoon Maldon sea salt

1 cup frozen petit pois

2 teaspoons peanut or other neutral oil

2 tablespoons butter

a light sprinkling of white wine (or tarragon) vinegar

2 scallions, trimmed and minced

grated zest and juice of ½ lime

1 heaping tablespoon chopped mint

freshly ground white pepper

Preheat the oven to 350°F. For the salad, tip the rice into a small, solid cooking pot that has a tight-fitting lid, add the water and salt, then bring up to a simmer. Tip in the peas, add the oil and butter, stir well, and return to a simmer. Put on the lid and cook in the oven for exactly 12 minutes.

On removing from the oven, leave the lid in place and allow to stand for 10 minutes. Now, sprinkle the vinegar over, fluff up the rice with a fork, lay a dish towel over the pan, and clamp it down with the lid. Leave for another 5 minutes. Tip out onto a tray to cool slightly. Add the rest of the ingredients, seasoning with plenty of pepper, stir, and pile onto a serving dish. Let cool.

To soft-boil the eggs, put them into a pan, cover with cold water, and bring to a boil, then switch off the heat, put on the lid, and leave them for 5 minutes to cook in the residual heat. Then, run cold water into the pan for about 3 minutes to halt the cooking. This should achieve a perfectly soft-boiled yolk, with a nicely set white. Carefully peel the eggs and place on the rice and pea salad.

Add the curry essence by degrees to the mayonnaise until you are happy with the taste. Spoon it over the eggs and garnish each one with a strip of roasted red pepper laid diagonally, lengthwise.

Croustade d'oeuf "Maintenon"

serves 4

◈ This is based upon a superb dish created by the great Michel Bourdin when he was chef at the Connaught Hotel, London. The original was made using quail eggs: *Croustade d'oeufs de cailles Maintenon* was its name then.

4 very fresh large eggs

splash of malt vinegar

for the pie crust

1 cup (scant) all-purpose flour

pinch of salt

6 tablespoons (¾ stick) butter, frozen

2 to 3 tablespoons ice-cold water, mixed with a generous squeeze of lemon juice

a little soft butter for greasing the pans

for the mushroom duxelles

3 tablespoons butter

4 shallots, peeled and chopped

¾ pound mushrooms, chopped, stalks and all

salt and freshly ground pepper

2 tablespoons Madeira

⅔ cup dry white wine

squeeze of lemon juice

2 teaspoons chopped tarragon

for the hollandaise sauce

3 large egg yolks

splash of water

1 cup (2 sticks) unsalted butter, melted, left to settle in the pan and kept warm

juice of ½ lemon

salt and freshly ground white pepper

To make the pie crust, put the flour and salt into a large bowl and, holding the butter with its wrapper, grate it into the flour, dipping the butter into the flour occasionally so that it doesn't become too sticky. Then gently turn the flour and butter around with a knife until all the flecks of butter are coated with flour and the mixture resembles lumpy bread crumbs. Now incorporate the lemon water, 1 tablespoon at a time, until the mixture gently comes together as a mass and leaves the bowl clean. Roll in a little extra flour and slip into a plastic bag. Refrigerate for 1 hour.

Preheat the oven to 350°F. Lightly butter 4 individual 4-inch tart pans, about 1¼ inches deep. Roll out the pie crust as thinly as you dare and use it to line the pans. Prick with a fork, line the pie crust with foil and dried beans, and bake blind in the oven for 20 minutes, or until crisp and a light golden color. Remove the foil and beans and leave the pie crust shells in the pans for 5 minutes after removing from the oven. Carefully unmold and keep warm on a plate in the residual heat of the switched-off oven, door ajar.

To make the duxelles, melt the butter in a pan and fry the shallots until golden. Add the mushrooms, season, and stew together until fairly dry, any juices from the mushrooms having been driven off. Add the Madeira and wine and simmer until they have reduced to almost nothing. Squeeze in the lemon juice, add the tarragon, and briefly pulse in a food processor to an evenly coarse purée; the mixture should not be smooth. Tip into a bowl, cover with a plate, and keep warm over a pan of simmering water.

To make the hollandaise, whisk the egg yolks with a splash of water until thick in a small stainless steel pan over very low heat, or a bowl over a pan of barely simmering water. Remove any scum from the surface of the butter and then add to the eggs in a thin stream, whisking constantly, until the consistency is similar to mayonnaise. Add the lemon juice and season. Keep warm.

Poach the eggs in simmering water, with the vinegar added, until slightly undercooked. Switch on the broiler.

To assemble, carefully spoon the duxelles into the pie crust shells and smooth the surface. Pop a poached egg on each and spoon the hollandaise over. Glaze for a few seconds under the hot broiler. Serve at once.

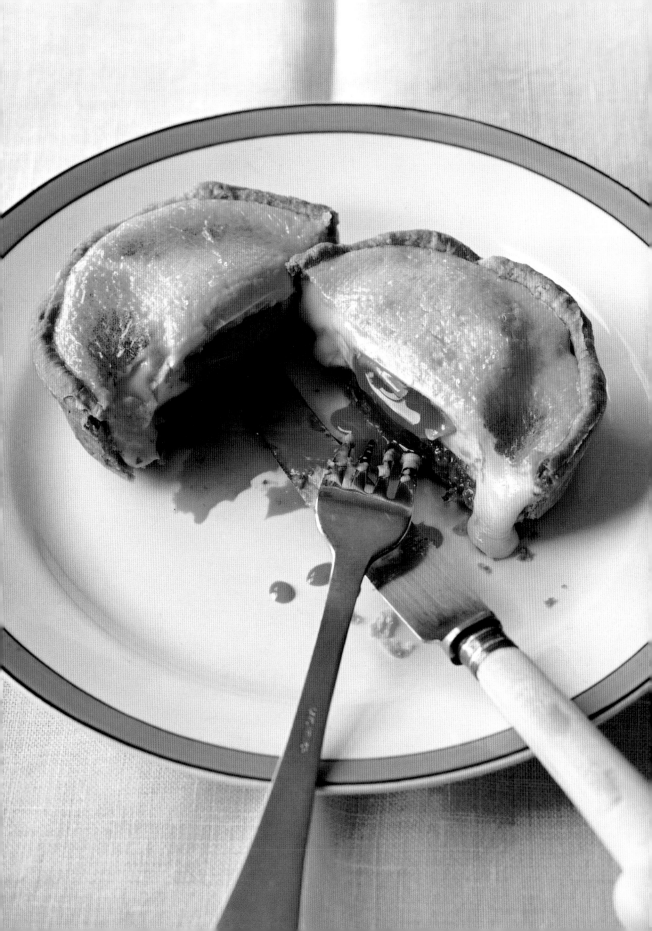

Omelette lyonnaise

serves I

To add extra texture and deliciousness to the omelet, you may like to add in some very tiny croutons just before the omelet is folded over. Without beating about the bush, this is a very buttery, but quite gorgeous omelet.

2 medium onions, about 1 pound in total, peeled

2 tablespoons butter, plus an extra 2 thin slices for cooking the omelet

3 medium eggs

salt and freshly ground pepper

2 teaspoons minced parsley

2 teaspoons red wine vinegar

Slice the onions very thinly. Melt the butter in a heavy-bottomed, small saucepan and cook the onions very gently until completely soft and just beginning to turn pale golden; this can take anything up to 30 minutes, so don't rush it and stir regularly. Allow to cool.

Beat the eggs with the seasoning and parsley, then stir in the onions. Melt a slice of butter in your favorite omelet pan and make the omelet in the usual way, tipping and tilting the pan so the runny egg finds the bottom of the pan where it may set; a spatula is useful here.

When the omelet is perfectly cooked, turn it out onto a warm plate, then quickly add the final slice of butter to the pan, cook until nut brown, then pour it over the omelet. In the still-hot pan, add the vinegar, swirl it around, and spoon it over the omelet. Eat at once.

Savory cheese custard with cream & chives

serves 4

❖ "Ethereal" might be an apt description, here, if not too presumptuous—or pretentious, even.

2 tablespoons butter, melted, to grease the molds

²⁄₃ cup (scant) Gruyère, grated

2½ tablespoons milk

²⁄₃ cup (scant) heavy cream

salt and freshly ground white pepper

3 large egg yolks

2 large whole eggs

1 to 2 tablespoons freshly grated Parmesan

for the cream and chive sauce

²⁄₃ cup whipping cream

3 tablespoons butter

1 tablespoon minced chives

salt and freshly ground pepper

Chill 4 dariole molds (preferably nonstick), about ²⁄₃-cup capacity. Preheat the oven to 300°F. Brush the inside of the chilled molds with the melted butter and put back into the refrigerator.

Put the Gruyère, milk, and cream into a pan over very gentle heat to melt the cheese, stirring constantly with a wooden spoon until smooth. Season to taste and then strain through a very fine strainer into a bowl. Let cool, then chill well in the refrigerator.

Once the mixture is cold, beat in the egg yolks and whole eggs and pass once more through a fine strainer. Fill the buttered molds with this mixture and stand them in a deep baking tray. Surround with lukewarm water to come two-thirds of the way up the side of the molds. Bake on the middle shelf of the oven for 45 to 50 minutes, or until firm to the touch.

Meanwhile, make the chive sauce. Gently simmer the cream and butter together for 3 to 4 minutes, until lightly thickened. Whisk vigorously until homogenized; keep warm.

Remove the timbales from the oven and leave them to rest for 5 minutes. Preheat the broiler.

Now carefully run a small knife around the edge of the molds and then gently invert into 4 lightly buttered, individual, shallow ovenproof dishes. Carefully sprinkle the surfaces of the timbales with the Parmesan, allowing a little to trail down the sides. Flash under the broiler briefly, to gild them. To serve, stir the chives into the sauce, season and pour around the timbales. Eat without delay.

Pene's celebrated cheese soufflé

serves 4

◈ My friend Pene cooks the best cheese soufflé. She and her husband, Albert, like to eat this little beauty for supper after having enjoyed a long lunch out. Having experienced such an occasion with them as their guest, I can only say how very sensibly some folk plan their day.

2½ tablespoons butter, plus extra to butter the dish

2 tablespoons all-purpose flour

1 cup (scant) low-fat milk

4 large egg yolks

5 large egg whites

1¼ cups grated sharp Cheddar

¼ cup grated Gruyère

¼ cup finely grated Parmesan, plus a little extra to finish

salt

generous pinch of cayenne pepper

Preheat the oven to 400°F. Thoroughly butter a 7-inch diameter soufflé dish, about 3 inches deep.

Melt the butter in a saucepan and mix in the flour. Cook together for a couple of minutes to make a roux, then gradually whisk in the milk until a smooth, very thick sauce is achieved. Remove from the heat and leave to cool slightly for a couple of minutes, then add the egg yolks one by one, beating them in thoroughly. Stir in the grated cheeses and season with salt and the cayenne. Pour into a roomy bowl, removing every last vestige of the mixture with a rubber spatula.

Whisk the egg whites in another bowl until firm. Stir a small amount into the cheese mixture to slacken it, then deftly fold in the rest of the whites, using a serving spoon or spatula.

Gently pile the mixture into the buttered soufflé dish and sprinkle the surface with extra Parmesan. Bake in the oven for 30 to 35 minutes, or until well risen, and golden and crusted on the surface.

Blueberries & Black Currants

Initially, I wasn't going to include desserts in this book. However, just because the book is concerned mainly with noncarnivorous savory delights, I felt that you, the reader, should not be deprived of some delightful desserts to finish with—and I love sweet things as much as anyone, both to eat and to cook. The only guideline I gave myself, nonetheless, was to limit the selection to a basis of fruit. I'm not quite sure why, but it just seemed more fitting, that's all.

I know that to munch on raw blueberries is probably the most healthy way of eating ever— or, at least, that is what we have been told by hale and hearty gurus the world over. However, the finest flavor of the blueberry and similar berries of the genus *Vaccinium*—whimberries (most heavily harvested in my home county, Lancashire), bilberries, whortleberries, and huckleberries—is when these dark little fruits have been cooked. Sugar and a touch of lemon juice are all that is necessary to bring out their hidden essence, although I have successfully used a powdered sweetener, instead of sugar when feeling ascetic.

Henry, a friend with whom I walk twice a week, swears by a large bowl of porridge, early every morning, and showers his serving with raw blueberries. I tell him that I can think of nothing more disgusting than to mix raw fruit of any kind with hot oatmeal: "It don't work!" I cry. "I make this little blueberry compote for my porridge and it is just lovely," I continue. "Too much of a chore," he says. Each, as ever, to their own, I guess . . .

Anyway, this compote really is dead simple to prepare: take $1\frac{1}{2}$ cups blueberries, 1 rounded tablespoonful of superfine sugar (about half that of sweetener), or to taste, and the juice of half a small lemon. Gently heat in a stainless steel pan until the berries burst and have exuded a modicum of juice. Cool them, or serve warm. The compote keeps well in the refrigerator for several days, too.

A black currant jelly has been on the menu at our restaurant Bibendum, in London, almost every day since we opened. It wobbles nicely and is served with crème Chantilly and warm, freshly baked madeleines. Everyone loves it. I cannot really give the original recipe here, however, as it contains nonvegetarian gelatin and will not turn out exactly the same when made with agar flakes. However, when set with this seaweed-based gelling agent, it does work as a wonderful, fruit layer in a recipe for trifle (see page 202).

Blueberry pie

serves 4

❖ Generally, when making a traditional, English fruit pie (crust both below and above), one does not add anything else to the filling except the fruit, sugar, and maybe a spice flavor, say. In contrast, an American fruit pie almost always includes a modicum of thickener (typically cornstarch), and several flecks of butter, too. I have, of late, warmed most generously to these new additions, as they add a pleasing extra richness, in the case of butter, and also, in the case of the cornstarch, prevent excess juice from pouring out of the pie while it cooks—as my mother's quite delicious whimberry pie used to do all over the bottom of the oven.

for the pie crust

4½ tablespoons (generous ½ stick) cold, unsalted butter, diced

4½ tablespoons (¼ cup, rounded) cold vegetable shortening (e.g. Crisco), cubed

1½ cups all-purpose flour

pinch of salt

2 to 3 tablespoons ice-cold water, to mix

a little milk for brushing

for the filling

2 tablespoons lemon juice

1 rounded tablespoon cornstarch

⅓ cup superfine sugar, plus a little extra for sprinkling

1 pound 2 ounces blueberries

several flecks of unsalted butter

To make the pie crust, put the fats, flour, and salt into a food processor and briefly process until resembling bread crumbs. Add enough water to form a dough and mix until well amalgamated. Knead lightly and chill in the refrigerator for at least 30 minutes. Cut off one-third of the dough for the top crust and rewrap it. Roll out the larger piece to an ⅛-inch-thick circle.

Preheat the oven to 400°F and place a baking sheet inside to heat up. Lightly grease an 8-inch-diameter loose-bottomed tart pan, about 1½ inches deep, and line with the pastry circle, allowing a little overhang. Prick the base several times with a fork.

For the filling, whisk together the lemon juice, cornstarch, and ⅓ cup sugar in a large bowl until smooth. Add the blueberries and turn all together with a spatula until the berries are well coated. Tip this into the pie shell and allow to settle. Disperse the butter flecks over the surface.

Roll out the other piece of pie crust to an ⅛-inch-thick circle. Brush the edge with a little milk and then flip the crust over the filling to form a lid. Tuck down around the outside of the fruit and press the edge onto the rim of the bottom crust to form a seal. Trim off excess pie crust with a sharp knife.

Brush the surface with milk and press the tines of a fork around the edge—for prettiness as much as anything. Make 3 small cuts in the center of the pie to allow steam to escape and sprinkle the surface generously with superfine sugar.

Slide the pie onto the baking sheet in the oven and bake for 10 minutes, then turn the temperature down to 350°F. Bake the pie for another 30 to 40 minutes, or until the surface is nicely crusted and golden. Serve at warm-to-room temperature for maximum enjoyment—and with some whipped cream or just a little heavy cream poured on top.

Black currant jelly trifle

serves 6

◈ I have used agar flakes here, to fulfill the vegetarian rule. If you would like to make the original jelly, you will find it in an earlier cookery book of mine, *Gammon & Spinach*.

for the black currant jelly

1¼ cups water

4 teaspoons agar flakes

3⅓ cups fresh or frozen black currants

1 cup (rounded) superfine sugar

¾ cup Port

for the other trifle layers

12 amaretti biscotti (i.e. 12 halves)

2 tablespoons crème de cassis

2 tablespoons Port

1 tablespoon Cognac

1¾ cups whipping cream

½ vanilla bean, split lengthwise

3 large egg yolks

1 large egg

1 rounded tablespoon superfine sugar

to finish

1¼ cups heavy cream

1 tablespoon confectioners' sugar

To make the jelly, put the water into a stainless steel pan and sprinkle the agar flakes over. Stir in and leave to soften for 5 minutes, then add the black currants, sugar, and Port. Bring up to a low simmer, cover, and cook for 10 minutes. Tip into a strainer suspended over a bowl. Leave to drain and drip for 30 minutes or so, then gently press upon the fruit with the back of a ladle to extract any final juices. Pour into 6 deep glass dishes and put in the refrigerator to set for at least 3 hours, or overnight, if you like.

Break up the amaretti biscotti into small pieces and mix them with the crème de cassis, Port, and Cognac. Allow the alcohols to be soaked up by the biscotti, then carefully spoon them over the surface of the jelly. Put back into the refrigerator.

To make the custard layer, heat the whipping cream with the vanilla bean, give it a quick whisk to disperse the vanilla seeds, cover, and leave to infuse. Beat the egg yolks and egg with the sugar. Strain the vanilla flavored cream over and mix together. Pour back into the cream pan and cook very gently over low heat, stirring constantly, until thickened. Be careful of overcooking, however, but be brave, because if the custard is not cooked enough, it will not be firm enough, once cold; you can safely take it as far as the occasional blip; when this happens, whisk vigorously to disperse the hot spots. Strain immediately into a bowl, cover, and cool completely.

Put the custard into the refrigerator to chill and thicken and then spoon it over the jelly and biscotti. Return to the refrigerator for 30 minutes.

Whip the cream with the confectioners' sugar until just holding peaks and pile on top of the trifle in a swirly way. Chill once more until ready to eat.

Raspberry crisp

serves 2

❖ For the best effect, I like to serve this crisp in individual, shallow dishes.

½ pound raspberries

sugar for sprinkling

several flecks of butter

for the crisp

½ cup (rounded) all–purpose flour

2½ tablespoons lightly salted butter

2 tablespoons sugar

Preheat the oven to 350°F. To make the topping, place all the ingredients in a big bowl and deftly rub them together until the mix is permeated with tiny bits of butter, among an otherwise sandy texture.

Divide the raspberries between 2 dishes, sprinkle with a little sugar, and dot with a few flecks of butter. Using a spoon, carefully cover with the topping, but do not be tempted to press it down. Dust with a little extra sugar.

Bake in the oven for 20 to 25 minutes, or until the topping is pale golden and the raspberry juice is gently bubbling. Serve warm, rather than piping hot.

Orange brûlée

serves 4

❖ To enjoy these brûlées at their best, serve them very cold.

finely pared zest of
1 large orange (no pith
whatsoever)

$^1\!/_2$ cup (rounded) superfine
sugar

1$^3\!/_4$ cups freshly squeezed
orange juice, strained

6 large egg yolks

1 cup (scant) crème fraîche

Using a small food processor, grind together the orange zest and $^1\!/_3$ cup of the sugar, until you have a bright orange paste.

Put the orange juice into a stainless steel pan, add the orange zest paste, bring up to a simmer, and reduce by half, to about 1 cup. Put to one side to cool for 15 minutes.

Whisk the egg yolks and crème fraîche together in a bowl, then whisk in the reduced orange mixture. Return to the pan and cook very gently over low heat until thickened to a custardlike consistency. Take care to avoid overcooking, but make sure the custard is cooked sufficiently, otherwise it will not be firm enough, once cold; you can safely take it as far as the occasional blip, and when this happens, whisk vigorously to disperse the hot spots.

Strain the custard immediately into 4 ramekins and cool completely, then chill in the refrigerator for at least 6 hours, preferably overnight.

Sprinkle the remaining sugar over the surface of the custards and caramelize under a preheated hot broiler, or using a cook's blowtorch, until melted, golden, and blistered in parts. Chill once more for 1 hour.

Eat with small teaspoons.

Baked quinces with maple syrup & white pepper

serves 2, with seconds

❖ There is a fairly rare *eau de vie de coing* (French for quince), of which a small amount may be added to some very cold, lightly sweetened whipped cream, to serve with these delicious quinces.

2 quinces, about 1¼ pounds

8 tablespoons pure maple syrup

1 tablespoon lemon juice

5 or 6 grindings of white pepper

Preheat the oven to 350°F. Cut the quinces lengthwise into quarters, using a sharp knife. Place in a lidded oven dish that will accommodate the pieces snugly. Pour the maple syrup and lemon juice over, and grind the pepper on top. Mix together with a spoon.

Put on the lid and bake in the oven for about 1 hour, occasionally turning the quinces through the syrup and basting, until they are tender and a gorgeous golden brown color. Serve warm, with whipped cream flavored as suggested above, if liked.

Damson & almond pudding cake

serves 4

❖ Essentially, deeply dark stewed fruit with a sponge top. If you cannot get damson plums, you can use another kind of plum.

8 tablespoons (1 stick) butter, softened, plus extra to grease the dish

1 pound damson plums, pitted

⅓ cup (rounded) superfine sugar

2 large eggs

1 teaspoon natural almond extract

¾ cup (scant) self-rising flour

⅓ cup ground almonds

½ teaspoon baking powder

pinch of salt

2 to 3 teaspoons confectioners' sugar

Preheat the oven to 350°F. Butter a presentable, fairly deep baking dish, strew with the pitted damsons, and cover them with 2 tablespoons of the butter, in flecks.

In a roomy bowl, beat the rest of the butter together with all the remaining ingredients, apart from the confectioners' sugar, until light and fluffy. Spoon this mixture over the damsons, slide into the oven, and bake for 40 minutes. If the surface of the pudding appears to be browning too quickly, turn the oven down to 310°F.

Sift the confectioners' sugar over the surface and bake for another 10 minutes, or so, until the sugar melts and becomes slightly crusted and the sponge is gently firm to a touch from the fingers. Leave to cool until warm, then eat with very cold cream poured on top.

Nuts & Nibbles

I have given nuts rather less recipe space than anticipated here. More than anything else, this is because of an association with the frightful "nut cutlet," one of the most infamous vegetarian options of all time. I have always loathed, really loathed, the masquerade of manufacturing vegetarian food, then using a moniker normally attached to something very well known indeed which has always been associated with meat products. The "Vegetarian burger." Please. "Vegetarian sausages." Just go away. Even meatless "sausage rolls." And, of course, that boneless—spineless, actually—"Nut cutlet."

A brief reasoning behind this book—there is more on this in the introduction—is absolutely *not* to disguise the fact that to eat happily, healthily, and deliciously it is not necessary to eat meat, poultry, and fish most of the time spent at table; the simple point is to enjoy noncarnivorous dishes, rather than be reminded of a contrary absence.

Nuts, of course, are full of protein—and fat, and carbohydrates, it should also be said—but it is well known that they are a healthful food, if eaten, like all such things, in moderation. Some people, as we know well, may not eat them due to allergy. And so severe can this be that health and safety laws now see it as their duty to announce on a package of nuts, that the package "contains nuts." How very efficient and helpful of them to warn us of this impending danger.

When it comes to cocktail parties, nuts are what less adventurous party givers will invariably choose to provide as "nibbles"—with, perhaps, olives as a secondary gesture to show a little effort. An astute comedian on the radio recently observed, however, that "there are always olives left in bowls the morning after, but all the bowls containing nuts are practically licked clean, so why don't we put out more nuts next time and just forget the olives?" Quite so.

Personally, I love making interesting nibbles, and those who eat them (wolf them, actually) are unable to resist, even though this is often preceded by mutterings of "Oh, I shouldn't, really" and "My diet is ruined" or, occasionally, "Yes please! I'm starving!" which is what you really want to hear and is very nice.

Homemade tiny rolls with white truffle paste

enough for about 40 rolls

◈ "Little soft slippers of eggy white bread with the most sublime and generous filling of white truffle paste smeared within" is how Terence Conran once described the inspiration for these: the *panini tartufati* offered at Procacci, in Florence.

Note that I suggest "spreadable" butter because if normal butter is used, the rolls, once cold, are firmer than one would wish for. White truffle paste may be purchased from good Italian food shops.

½ cup milk

4 tablespoons (½ stick) "spreadable" butter

1 teaspoon Maldon sea salt

1½ teaspoons sugar

2⅓ cups bread flour

2 teaspoons quick–rise yeast

1 large egg, beaten

to finish the rolls

1 small egg, beaten with a little milk and a pinch of salt

to serve

unsalted butter

white truffle paste

Put the milk, butter, salt, and sugar into a pan and heat until just warm to the finger. Put to one side. In a large bowl or electric food mixer, mix together the flour, yeast, and beaten egg. Add the milk mixture and blend in with the flour until it has become a dough (occasionally, the mixture is a touch sticky, but once kneading begins, a little extra flour added will rectify this).

Knead for 10 minutes or so, until nicely soft and supple. Put into a large, lightly greased bowl, cover with a damp dish towel, and allow to rise somewhere warm, for about 1 hour, or until doubled in size.

Preheat the oven to 450°F. Lightly grease a flat baking tray. Tip the risen dough onto a floured counter, punch it down, and then knead for a moment or two. Now begin to break off small pieces of dough and set them to one side until all the dough is exhausted.

Form the pieces of dough into little balls, then roll these into tiny torpedo shapes: i.e. slightly higher in the middle than they are at each end, and with a smooth top. As you shape each one, place on the baking tray, spacing them about ¾ inch apart (once they have risen, they should just be touching each other). Cover with a light and flimsy dry dish towel and, once again, place somewhere warm, to rise for a second time, for around 40 minutes, or until more than doubled in size.

Now then, for the brave of heart, this is the time you very lightly brush them with the beaten egg/milk/salt mixture. Occasionally, the rolls are so well risen and light, that the merest touch can, maddeningly, deflate them. If you are at all nervous about this, then brush them before they rise; the finished result will not be quite as beautiful, but at least you will have them perfectly baked!

Anyway, whichever route you take, bake for about 8 minutes on an upper shelf of the oven, but not the topmost one, until golden on top and smelling absolutely wonderful. Cool on a wire rack.

Split lengthwise, spread with unsalted butter, and slather with truffle paste. Sandwich back together and eat with a glass of the finest white wine you can afford. Finally, do try to eat all of them at their very best—on the day of baking.

Potato fritters with sesame & pine nuts

makes about 20

❖ Offer these either as a small nibble, or as a dish in themselves with, say, a salad of fine green beans.

1 pound waxy potatoes, such as Yukon Gold, peeled and cut into chunks

for the choux paste

½ cup (scant) water

1½ tablespoons butter

salt and freshly ground white pepper

⅓ cup (rounded) all-purpose flour

2 large eggs

1 large egg yolk

to finish

flour for coating

2 to 3 tablespoons sesame seeds

3 to 4 tablespoons pine nuts

1 egg, loosely beaten

oil for deep-frying

Steam the potatoes until tender, then allow to dry out a little. Pass them through a food mill or potato ricer, onto a sheet of waxed paper or a tray. Leave to cool.

Meanwhile, make the choux paste: boil together the water, butter, and seasoning in a saucepan. Take off the heat, tip in the flour all at once, and beat together, using a wooden spoon, until thoroughly combined and very smooth. Now, one by one, start to beat in the eggs and egg yolk, making sure that each one has been fully incorporated before adding the next one. The final result should be a glossy, stiff yellow paste. Beat this thoroughly into the dry potato until the mixture is smooth. Spread into a shallow dish, cover with plastic wrap, and put into the refrigerator to firm up.

Using floured hands or 2 teaspoons, take small amounts of the mixture and form into balls the size of a small-ish walnut. Roll them in flour and put onto a tray. Mix together the sesame seeds and pine nuts and spread them out onto another tray. Now pass each potato ball through beaten egg and then roll them through the seeds and nuts, making sure of a good covering.

Heat the oil in the deep fryer to 190°F and cook the fritters in 2 or 3 batches for about 3 to 4 minutes, until crisp and golden. Keep warm in a very low oven, on double folded paper towels, while you continue with the next batch.

Very good eaten with mayonnaise that has had some chili sauce stirred into it.

Caerphilly cheese croquettes

makes about 12 to 15

◈ These little croquettes are best served warm.

5 ounces grated Caerphilly or Cheddar cheese

3 cups (rounded) fresh white bread crumbs

2 tablespoons minced scallion

3 large egg yolks

1 tablespoon chopped parsley

1 teaspoon mustard powder

salt and freshly ground pepper

a little milk (if needed)

oil for deep–frying

flour for coating

1 large egg, loosely beaten

Mix together the cheese, half of the bread crumbs, and scallion. In a bowl, whisk the egg yolks, parsley, mustard, and seasoning together and add the bread crumb and cheese mixture to make a firm paste; if the mix is too sloppy, add a little more bread crumbs; if too dry, add a little milk.

Form the mixture into little cork shapes and place on a floured tray. Put in the refrigerator to firm up for about an hour.

When ready to cook, heat the oil for deep-frying in a suitable pan to about 190°F. Put the flour, the beaten egg, and the remaining bread crumbs into 3 separate shallow dishes.

Firstly, roll the croquettes in flour, then egg, and, finally, bread crumbs. Deep-fry in the hot oil for 3 to 4 minutes, or until a pale golden color and nice and crisp. Drain on paper towels and serve.

"Ajo verde"

serves 2 to 3

◈ I have taken the liberty of turning the cold Spanish garlic and almond soup, *ajo blanco*, into one that is pale green, sweet, and lightly spiced with a little green chili. I hope you like it.

5 ounces pistachios, skinned

⅓ cup extra–virgin olive oil, plus a trickle to serve

½ cucumber (¼ pound)

1 green chili

6 ounces seedless green grapes

1½ cups water

5 or 6 garlic cloves, peeled and crushed

1½ teaspoons Maldon sea salt

10 mint leaves

3 to 4 teaspoons sherry vinegar, or to taste

juice of 1 small lime

croutons, to serve

In a nonstick skillet, lightly toast the pistachios in 1 teaspoon of the oil, coloring them hardly at all. Leave to cool, then tip into a blender.

Peel and roughly chop the cucumber, seed and chop the chili, and add both to the blender with all the other ingredients. Process until very smooth indeed, then pass through a fine strainer into a bowl, pressing down on the solids to extract every last vestige of liquid.

Chill thoroughly in the refrigerator for at least 4 hours. Serve in chilled soup bowls, and with super-crisp tiny croutons. I also like to add one cube of ice to each serving and a tiny trickle of best olive oil, too.

Very good as a summer appetizer when served in iced shot glasses.

Rachel Cooke's wonderful Parmesan crackers

makes about 25 to 30

❖ I first tasted these extraordinarily delicious crackers at Rachel and her husband Tony's North London home. They were served with an equally delicious bottle of Champagne, which, in turn, preceded a dinner of a familiar spiced eggplant salad, with a very fine roast chicken to follow. These occasional dinners with particular friends revolve around the consumption of a few fine bottles. So some excellent red wine was poured, we moved on to slices of ripe cheese . . . and at that moment, I felt that all was really quite all right with the world. Silly old Hop.

6½ tablespoons (generous ¾ stick) cold, unsalted butter, cut into chunks

¾ cup (scant) all-purpose flour

pinch of salt

pinch of cayenne pepper

½ heaping teaspoon mustard powder

⅓ cup (rounded) finely grated Cheddar

⅓ cup (rounded) finely grated Parmesan, plus a little extra to finish

1 large egg, beaten

Preheat the oven to 350°F. Put the butter and flour into a food processor, together with the salt, cayenne pepper, mustard powder, and cheeses. Briefly process all together to begin with, and then, finally, pulse the mixture in short spurts as you notice the mixture coming together—as pastry, if you like. Once the texture is clearly "clumpy," tip it all out onto a lightly floured counter and deftly, but thoroughly, knead it together until well blended and smooth. Wrap in plastic wrap and chill in the refrigerator for at least 30 minutes.

Gently roll out the pastry on a lightly floured counter to about an ⅛-inch thickness. Using a 1½ to 2-inch cookie cutter, cut out crackers the size you wish for, depending on the occasion. Lay them out onto a greased baking tray about ¾ inch apart; it may be necessary to bake them in 2 batches.

Carefully brush the surface of each cracker with beaten egg and sprinkle a little finely grated Parmesan over. Bake in the oven for 10 minutes, or until a gorgeous, pale golden color is achieved; the superb smell will also inform you that they are ready. Carefully lift off the tray using a spatula and place on a cooling rack. Serve while still just warm, if possible.

French 75 & Other Cocktails

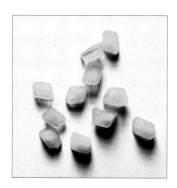

In my view it is Italian bartenders, and most often on their home ground, who make the finest, most pure and traditional cocktails anywhere. These genial, knowing fellows also present themselves most elegantly in their pressed white linen jackets, black trousers, and brilliant white shirts with thin black (not bow) ties. They are a lesson to all would-be practitioners of the art of mixing a good drink.

One feels relaxed and confident when observing such people at work, rather than becoming stressed, as I do, sitting on my stool and watching the simplest cocktail go from bad to worse in a matter of minutes, even in the heart of London's Mayfair.

The pretty and, I modestly think, delicious Hoppy's Pink is my only real attempt at cocktail creation here, with the other ones merely touched by personal interpretation. The drink has its origins in the Pink Gin, which was particularly popular in the British Navy pre- and post- the Second World War, but which has now almost disappeared without trace. This is due, of course, to a slew of the filthiest, overcomplicated cocktails ever offered to the serious barfly in modern times. Why, pray, would you ever wish to add chocolate to a Martini?

Anyways, as they might say in the more louche bars of Manhattan, this pink drink is a lovely, if potent, early evening summer cocktail.

If you wish, a small splash of Campari gives the drink an even pinker color and also adds a pleasing touch of bitterness.

Firstly, however, here is a classic—and relatively new to me, I might add. First imbibed in the Bar Hemingway of the Paris Ritz.

French 75

makes 2 drinks

❖ In summertime, you can serve this as a long drink if you prefer—over ice in highball glasses and garnished with a sprig of mint.

2½ ounces gin (ideally Plymouth)

2½ ounces lemon juice, strained

3 to 4 teaspoons superfine sugar

nonvintage Champagne, chilled

Using a long spoon, mix together the gin, lemon juice, sugar, and several ice cubes in a pitcher and stir well. Strain into 2 large, chilled flutes and fill up with Champagne.

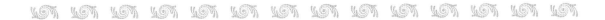

Hoppy's pink

makes 2 drinks

❖ My singular attempt at cocktail creation.

2½ ounces gin or vodka

4 drops Angostura bitters

1 to 2 teaspoons superfine sugar, to taste

3½ ounces freshly squeezed pink grapefruit juice, strained

7 ounces pink Champagne, chilled

1 pink grapefruit slice, halved

Using a pitcher, briefly mix together the gin or vodka, bitters, sugar, and grapefruit juice, over ice. Strain into 2 large wine glasses, with 5 cubes of ice in each. Fill up with Champagne, stir carefully, add the sliced grapefruit, and serve promptly.

Correct Pimms

makes 1 moderate pitcherful, enough for 2 or 3

❖ I absolutely loathe Pimms when it resembles fruit salad. This is not that.

4 ounces Pimms No. 1

2 ounces gin

3 or 4 orange slices

3 or 4 lemon slices

4 or 5 mint sprigs

3 or 4 strips cucumber skin

10 ounces lemon soda, chilled

Mix everything together well in a pitcher with plenty of ice cubes, leave to infuse for 2 to 3 minutes, then pour into glasses containing more ice. Garnish each glass with mint and an extra slice of orange and lemon, if desired.

Jalapeño bloody Mary

makes 1 small pitcherful, enough for 2 or 3 glasses

❖ Here you can, of course, use my vegetarian version of Worcestershire sauce (see page 81).

2 or 3 jalapeño chilis

1¼ cups tomato juice

2½ ounces vodka

1½ ounces dry sherry

2 teaspoons Worcestershire sauce

1 teaspoon Tabasco

juice of 1 small lime

large pinch of celery salt

Roughly chop the chilis and add to the tomato juice. Leave to infuse for at least 24 hours.

Strain the juice through a strainer into an ice-filled pitcher and add everything else. Stir well and strain into small, chilled tumblers.

Index

Acknowledgements I would like to thank... Jane O'Shea, Jason Lowe, Lawrence Morton and Clare Lattin... for, respectively, their encouragement and support; enthusiasm and artistry; unique style and charm; holding my hand, yet again... And, especially, Janet Illsley, for her exacting editorial skills and endless patience with my particular verbiage. Finally, as ever, my fondest regard for Anthony Goff, who has been my loyal agent for 25 years.

First published in 2009 by Quadrille Publishing Limited
Published in 2010 by Stewart, Tabori & Chang
An imprint of ABRAMS

Text copyright © 2009 Simon Hopkinson
Photographs copyright © 2009 Jason Lowe

All rights reserved. No portion of this book may be reproduced, stored in a retrieval system, or transmitted in any form or by any means, mechanical, electronic, photocopying, recording, or otherwise, without written permission from the publisher.

Library of Congress Cataloging-in-Publication Data

Hopkinson, Simon (Simon G.)
  The vegetarian option / Simon Hopkinson ; pictures by Jason Lowe.
    p. cm.
  Includes index.
  ISBN 978-1-58479-847-7
  1. Vegetarian cookery. I. Title.
  TX837.H693 2010
  641.5'636--dc22
                    2009045551

Publishing director Jane O'Shea
Creative director Helen Lewis
Project editors Janet Illsley and Eleanor Van Zandt
Art direction & design Lawrence Morton
Photographer Jason Lowe
Stylist Cynthia Inions
Production director Vincent Smith
Production controller Ruth Deary
Editorial Assistant Sarah Jones

The text of this book was composed in Musee and Prelo.

Printed and bound in China
10 9 8 7 6 5 4 3 2 1

Stewart, Tabori & Chang books are available at special discounts when purchased in quantity for premiums and promotions as well as fundraising or educational use. Special editions can also be created to specification. For details, contact specialsales@abramsbooks.com or the address below.

THE ART OF BOOKS SINCE 1949

115 West 18th Street
New York, NY 10011
www.abramsbooks.com